I0473174

First Printing

ISBN 978-1467999243

www.ereselling.com

# You Can Sell it!

## By: Ryan Andes

*"Far better it is to dare mighty things, to win glorious triumphs, though checkered with failure; than to rank among those poor souls who neither enjoy much nor suffer much; because they live in the grey twilight that knows neither victory nor defeat"*

*~Teddy Roosevelt*

# Table of Contents

# Introduction

First I would like to thank you for your purchase and I hope this will offer you much enlightenment in the world of sales and inspire the inner greatness in you. This book has been written for and is intended to be read by anyone with an interest in work at home income and an entrepreneur spirit. This includes the person who has never sold anything to the person who has been selling their entire life.

Over the last ten years I have perfected the art of resale and learned how to maximize profits while minimizing risk and losses. My online sales over this time have exceeded one million dollars and over 20,000 sales. I have had to overcome great adversity in my life on many occasions to get to where I am today. I realize many of you may have had to go through financially difficult times and maybe you are going through that right now. I am here to tell you NEVER GIVE UP! Dig deep down and find the strength and the will to keep moving forward no matter how tough times are, if you never give up than you will never fail! I offer the next part below to possibly inspire you or motivate you to make some money and believe that you can be successful in whatever you do. If you are already successful in life or you just don't care about my background than skip this below and move on to Chapter 1.

At the age of 19 I was flat broke and I found myself in quite a predicament, as an irresponsible teenager I had just gotten a DWI and lost my license and was facing some expensive fines and lawyer fees as well as other bills adding up.

I was a poor college student living at home and my parents were so angry at me they were about to kick me out. I needed to come up with close to $3000 in 45 days and I had nobody to turn to for help and no license to look for a job. I had a girlfriend of six months at the time who lived 30 miles away from me and she did not have a car and my future was not looking too bright.

My back was against the wall and it felt like the world was going to crush me, I felt hopeless and worthless and my mind was racing and then my sadness turned into anger. I went to my room and punched the walls and knocked over everything I could. After a few hours of anger I began to settle down and started thinking of ways I could make some money and decided to search the internet as you may have very well done to find this handbook. I saw an ad for eBay, an online auction site and clicked on it to see what was being sold on there. Keep in mind this was the year 2001 and eBay did not have the popularity it enjoys today. I noticed people were listing and selling just about everything and anything and at good prices. I was intrigued immediately and a spark went off in me and the feeling of hope returned. I ran through my house for about an hour trying to find anything I thought would be of value that I could part with, and anything I thought my parents would not miss or notice was gone (I don't recommend that last part – always get permission before selling anything that is not yours!).

My pile of items included my Fender Stratocaster electric guitar and amplifier with accessories, my old sporting equipment, board games, Super Nintendo & Nintendo 64 video game systems, old college books, tools I found in the garage and my car CD player head unit (I wasn't going to be driving for awhile so I didn't think I would miss it for awhile). I borrowed my mother's digital camera and worked through the night taking pictures and writing down descriptions.

I used the basic listing service on the eBay website and managed to list close to twenty five items on the auction site. Keep in mind that after I finished each listing it automatically was listed on eBay so my first listing went on around 6:30 PM and my last item went on around 1:00 AM which is a terrible time to be listing items for auction because they will end at the same time they are listed and not many people are online then. I will get into listing and best practices later in the book.

Seven days later I had sold close to $1500, reaching half of my target funds that I needed. I had no idea how to ship them out, at first I found boxes around the house and used tissue paper, old clothes and even blankets to ship out the first bit of items. This soon ran out and I ended up getting a friend to take me to a local pack and ship store to handle the rest. The pack and ship stores are extremely convenient but they charge outrageous prices for shipping and can kill your profits quickly. Needless to say after my first week of sales a fire was lit inside me, I saw my neighbor was having a yard sale and explained to him my situation for raising money and he cut me a deal and I ended up buying close to twenty items for about a hundred bucks including a nice set of golf clubs. I asked a few friends if they needed to sell anything and was surprised at their eagerness to provide me with head units, stereos, game systems and other items they were going to toss out or didn't need any more. You really may be surprised if you just ask around at the amount of items you can find to sell. With the items I got at the yard sale and profits from my friends sales (I split the profits with them) I checked my PayPal account and there was a little over $5,000! I had done it and needless to say when my friends heard about my success the items just kept flowing in.

A few months later after paying my mines are getting my license back I decided to partner up with two friends in a business venture to sell online.

We rented out a warehouse that was beat up and in a very bad section of the city in Baltimore, Maryland but we had access to 50,000 square feet of space and the rent was only $300 with the requirement that we help sell the companies second hand inventory they had in their many warehouses. We started networking with other salesmen in the area and business associates and built a very fast network of consignment clients. One of our best was with a local junk removal company, they would get paid to remove all kinds of things from estates, unwanted personal items, cleanouts, etc and we had no trouble splitting the profits right down the middle considering they were being paid to take the items. The first year our sales were a modest $187k and we decided to hire a few college kids for shipping and handling to free up our time and a sales manager to oversee daily management activities. We hired a few more employees and paid them on commission which made their hiring and payment a low risk situation given they were properly trained and reliable. We were really on a roll, some months we would pull in $50,000, our sales for the year were over $500k with just a small force of employees.

The next year would be my best and worst of my life; it started out amazing with sales off the charts. We merged with another local eBay company that had several local package and ship stores under contract as eBay drop off stores. We would buy out another small company shortly after with the same business model and expand the number of stores we had under contract to fifteen and most were operational excepted items from their local customer base. We had plans to have fifty more stores under contract by the end of the year, and then eventually spread out throughout the east coast and then all of the United States.

One of the co-owners and I created a software solution with a web interface and backend databases to process eBay drop off customers items and link all the stores together to manage sales and accounting. The solution enabled the owners of the drop off locations to input pictures, descriptions and give us shipping prices so when we sold one of these items all we had to do was tell the drop off location where the item was to be shipped to and they handled it. They even stored the items at their locations so we did not have to worry about lost items, returns and security of the item, the liability was completely on them. Sales were booming, we established a board of directors and I located a company that would act as a "market maker" and help my company go public and be traded on the open market. Not the NASDAQ or NYSE, just the OTCBB but this was still a huge move for my company. I was 23 years old, I had just purchased a new RX-8 and a Honda Civic Hybrid, moved into the best apartment money could buy, had 60k in the bank, I was going out to fancy restaurants with CEOs, Politian's, and millionaires. I was planning my future and family with my girlfriend, my best friends were also some of my employees and co-owners who I got to see and hang out with everyday. Life was perfect!

As quick as I climbed to the top of the business world, it would crumble and fall in what seemed like an instant. The warehouse that we had been renting and using as our central office as well as still handling lots of consignment contracts was filled with inventory. Within a month we were robbed twice and then to top it off somebody stole a car and torched the evidence on the side of our warehouse burning our warehouse to the ground. We were lied to by the company we rented the building from as they stated all along that our company was covered under their insurance which it would turn out we were not.

We had sold and not yet shipped close to $20k worth of inventory that went up in flames, another $100k worth of inventory was lost, and all of our servers and equipment were destroyed. Every employee we had working at the warehouse either quit or we had to let go. The board of directors started fighting with each other about how to move forward; after all we still had our drop off locations operational. After losing our warehouse and those employees who were listing our inventory online we could not keep up with orders, our reputation was hurt, not to mention we were being sued for losses and damages from the consignees whose items went up in flames. We had to process fifty or so refunds on eBay left many very angry buyers who in turn left very bad feedback killing our main eBay sales account. I would end up dishing out over $40k of my own money to try and keep the company going by paying salaries and handling operational costs but in the end it was a losing battle.

I ended up taking on too much debt, as did the company and within a few short months the company was bankrupt. In turn not to many months later I too was bankrupted, evicted from my apartment, had my cars repossessed, bank accounts closed. I let my girlfriend of four years go in a selfless act as I could not let her go down with me, and I was ashamed and embarrassed of what had happened to me and who I became. I moved bank into my parents house a broken man with virtually nothing to live for. So, I ask the question again, are you going through a tough time in your life? I assure you I have felt your pain, having had everything I could of ever dreamed in life one moment and than having it all taken from me in the next. I wanted to find that guy who said "You don't know what you got, till it's gone" and beat him senseless.

This would be the lowest point of my previously beloved life, so what did I do? I got back up on my feet and started back at the beginning selling what possessions I had and those of friends and family and within a few years I had risen from the ashes like a phoenix, paid off my debts, put myself through college and saved up enough money to where I could start a business again or travel the world without worrying about money.

I share my brief story of failure and success with you because I want to help, I want to motivate and inspire greatness in everyone I come in contact with. I wrote this book as a way to try and give something back to the community and try to be a beacon of light. I also want to shed any doubt of any scams that are out there, I have been taken advantage of a few times myself by make money schemes and tricks. There are no tricks or scams here, you won't be a millionaire tomorrow by applying the principles of my knowledge I assure you of that, and if you are, you must let me know what you did differently! It is worth noting that completing this book is a massive feat for someone like me, I have serious

ADHD and I get bored very easily and have a hard time staying in one place for more than twenty minutes so you can imagine how long this journey has taken me. Writing and reading are not fun task for me and I have great difficulty focusing and I will admit that there is only one book that I have read in its entirety and that was the wonderful work of Robert Kiyosaki's "Rich Dad, Poor Dad" which if you have not read you need to pick yourself up a copy! If you have stuck with me this long through the introduction I thank you, now let's make some money!

# Chapter 1 – Getting Started

Before we get started buying & selling and thinking about retirement there are some things we need to prepare first. You will need to establish your starting bankroll, basically figure out how much money you are going to allocate to get started, than create a budget. This should be disposable income, especially for those just starting out because you may make some costly mistakes, so don't use your rent money to get started! What I typically do is withdraw $5,000 every month that I am going to use for purchasing inventory; my target return when I am making purchases is three times what I spend. My monthly target is usually $10,000 profit, so therefore I need to make sure I spend my $5,000 on inventory and I can hit my goal. Don't be discouraged by the numbers, you should be getting a much greater return if you are buying lower cost items than higher ones. Here is my basic spending principles that have treated me well; If I buy an item for $5 I need to be getting 5 to 1 on my money or it just simply is not worth my time and trouble. For example if I see a Nintendo Gameboy it might be worth $25 on Amazon but I am not going to bother bidding on it if it goes above the $5 mark, you need to leave yourself room for profit.

There may be something wrong with the item and if you're potential return does not justify the risk of more profit than you need to simply pass it up and move on to the next item. Again, this is only a guideline, if you know that there is a guarantee that the item you are buying will sell all day long at $25 and there is no risk of damage to the item and your ok with making a small profit, go ahead and spend the $10 on it. Sometimes when you're at a tough auction or sale and you can't get anything at the right price but you can buy a large quantity of items and only double your money, go for it if you're ok with the return. Moving on with my return guidelines, buying an item for $10-$15 it is good to try and get 4 to 1, when moving up to $20-$50 items I like to try and get 3 to 1. The $75-$150 range at least 2.5 to 1 and $200-$500 is when I start looking at just doubling my money and when you start getting higher up such as spending $2000 on an item (maybe a car, or jewelry, antique weapons, rare coins, etc) it is ok to start taking smaller percentage returns because the dollar values justify the spending. I can remember spending close to $2,000 (including buyers' premium and tax which I was aware of when bidding) on a rare Carson City Morgan Silver Dollar that I knew I could sell for a minimum of $2,500, I ended up selling it for $2,900. After fees I was looking at a $700 profit, which is not too bad for an hour's work. It becomes obvious of the difference of percentages you are expecting when the value goes up, at the same rate it would not be wise to spend $20 on an item you expected to sell for only $25.

If you are just starting out I recommend buying mostly $5-$10 items and a lot of them so you can minimize your variance, maximize your returns, build your bankroll and not tie up to much of your spending cash. Don't automatically assume if you're buying items for $5 that you're not going to make any money and you're wasting your time. Be aggressive and take chances, don't be caught waiting on the sidelines at an auction for one or two specific items or not pulling the trigger when you have the chance and somebody else grabs your item. Buy and bid with confidence!

Many people come up to me asking for help getting started but they don't think they have enough money to get started. The philosophy that it takes money to make money is simply WRONG!

When I was in my hay day as CEO I was also an investor and I was part of a group of real estate investors, known as Investors United and I watched members of their group make millions, yes millions of dollars without putting out a cent. They would find people interested in selling their homes and sometimes in desperate need of money, than they would have them sign a real estate contract and gave them rights to buy the home. The investors would than sell the house at public auction, pay off the seller of the home and pocket the profits. There are many ways we can use similar techniques to sell items on the internet. For starters do you have neighbors or family members that might want to get rid of stuff that you could potentially sell for them?  Maybe they want to sell a car for $2000 that you know is worth at least $3000 but you don't have the capital to buy it, what a shame right? Most people would walk away from the opportunity but not you, you're too creative so you write up a simple contract or verbal agreement if you trust them to give you the exclusive right to buy the car for the next 30 days. It is always best to be honest and upfront with your intentions, most people are reasonable and are willing to leave you a little on the table if you explain the situation, sure you could just try and find a buyer without talking to them first but they might not react as favorable as you hope to what you have done and might cut your out of the deal entirely. So after you have a deal in place with the seller you decide to put ads in the newspaper, craigslist, auto trader and eBay for the car at $3500 OBO. You find a buyer willing to pay your asking price and he writes you a check for the money, you pay whoever you were selling the car for the $2000 they wanted and you pocket the rest, guess what you just brokered your first deal!

There are other ways of getting starting capital if you're not interested in consignment or selling personal items and you have no extra money. Do you own a credit card? While many people are scared of using their credit cards and getting hit with interest payments, this can be a viable solution. You have 30 days before interest will begin accruing on your spending which is more than enough time to flip a few items and repay your debt before you owe any interest. If you can't resell the items in 30 days does it really matter? Even if your APR is 20% and you spend $500 on the credit card you are only going to pay interest for one month which would be about 1.6% of $500, so now you owe $508. If you can't beat the low interest rates of a credit card flipping inventory something is seriously wrong.

I understand the concept of taking on debt scares many people and if you can't force yourself to do this, or you are worried about losing sleep at night over debt than don't do it. Instead consider family members, friends or other trustworthy people you know who might have a little bit of extra cash lying around. Don't simply ask them to borrow money, tell them what you plan to do with it, offer them a percentage return. You're helping them out now by putting their money to work and providing a winning solution for both parties. Early in my business days my business partner and I did not have the capital to make the deal of the century, a local scuba shop had gone out of business and we had the chance to purchase their entire remaining inventory and the asking price was $21,000. After doing our due diligence (proper research and analysis of the situation) we were able to calculate a minimum return of the listed inventory to be $50000. The inventory was all brand new and top of the line, and looking at the market for such equipment we knew it would be a very fast turn over. We presented this information to my business partner's father who was very wealthy by this time in his life. We presented him with projected sales figures, our past sales history and turnover rate and he was ready to sign a check. We promised him a return of at least $23000 in 60 days; we paid him $25000 in 40 days. Needless to say after that we knew we had a confident investor for any future deals. The point of this deal is that you should not be immediately scared off by high numbers, if there is the potential for money to be made all you need is the will to make it happen.

## What to look for?

When you are first starting out it is usually a good idea to focus on what you already know if applicable. You don't need to be an expert, as I don't consider myself an expert on any particular type of item. I do however know a lot about a lot of different types of items, and more importantly I know the value of them. I have been told before that if I ever got on the price is right I would be accused of cheating. If you are inexperienced in sales or pricing stick to what you know, maybe a hobby of yours or just something that you are very interested in. Maybe you like to work on cars; maybe you love photography or collect coins and money. Perhaps you're a sports nut and you know the big names on sports teams, you could also be a computer nerd and I don't mean that to be offensive as I consider myself one as well as a sports nut.

Regardless if you can find something you already know about and are interested in, it will make it easier and you will be more confident in buying and selling these types of items. When I get asked what type of items I sell, my response is anything I can make a profit on. I do however love buying and selling cameras, antique clocks, musical instruments and electronics and that is usually the first types of items I look for when I am out hunting. If you are trying to make some extra money or turn reselling into a nice hobby and supplemental income it is a lot easier to focus on a niche category you like, however if you are trying to do it for a living you may want to expand your product base. There is no reason to worry about what to look for yet, or worry that you don't know anything about item values. I am going to show you a few techniques that I use to make myself feel like an expert and give me the confidence to make smart purchases.

# Research and Valuation of items

I am going to reveal my most valuable secret when it comes to buying or bidding. Unlike my competition I almost NEVER lose money on items that I purchase. Whenever I am given the opportunity to view an item before bidding or buying I don't rely on guessing or what I think something sold for somewhere or a price I read in a guide that is most likely outdated by now. I carry a small note pad with me and a pen and I try and write down a brief but informative description about the item. The first thing I look for is the brand name, the next thing is the model or catalog number, brief description of what the item is and possibly a serial number if I am going to have time to do extensive research or if it even applies.

For instance, if you are looking up a Fender Stratocaster guitar you will find an overwhelming number of results and prices ranging all over the place. However if you have a serial number you will be able to track down the year of the guitar in question and have a better shot at getting the price range of the one in question. If I can't find a model number, serial number, brand name or any identifying marks on the item which will be the case for many antiques than I try to be as descriptive as possible with the item. What is the item made of? About how long is it? What color is it? The other day I saw a spoon and fork deco set and was not sure of the value. They wooden, very large and looked to be rather old, I did research on the keywords vintage/antique wooden huge/large spoon/fork and found a lot of comparable results.

Typically I will write down descriptions for items that I am not familiar with, items that appear to be potentially valuable which is going to be different for everyone but you get a better idea the longer you do it. I also like to write down the condition to the best of my knowledge, if something is missing parts or pieces that I can tell or scratched, cracked or damaged in any way I will note it. Check if the battery compartment is corroded, if it is electrical then plug it into an outlet if possible to see if it powers on. The more information you can get the better your decision process will be and the more accurate your price evaluation will be. This process is known as due diligence, if you don't do your due diligence than you will have only yourself to blame for stupid purchases and lost money. The amount of information that I write down for a specific item depends on how long I will have to do research and how many items I am interested in.

After I have written down my descriptions and am satisfied with them I go back to my car. I have a netbook with a paid wireless anywhere service that allows me to access the internet just about anywhere in the United States. When I have several pages full of items to lookup and want the fastest research possible I use www.terapeak.com which is authorized and promoted by eBay, Market Research database. This site will allow you to pull up all of the sold and unsold results for an item listed on eBay for any 90 day period within the previous year. So let's say we are at an estate sale of a rich camera collector and there is a Leica M9 Camera in mint condition there that the estate company has verified to be authentic. We plug in Leica M9 camera into Terapeak for the last 90 days of sales. Below are the results:

| | Item Title | Sold | Format | Start Price | End Price ▼ | Bids | End Date |
|---|---|---|---|---|---|---|---|
| | Leica M9 Black Full Frame 18mp Camera W/ Accessories | Yes | FBN | $6,995.00 | $6,995.00 | 1 | 2011-04-21 |
| | Leica M9 18 Megapixel Steel Gray Digital Camera - NEW | Yes | 📷 | $6,995.00 | $6,995.00 | 1 | 2011-03-21 |
| | Leica M9 GREY Full Frame 18mp Rangefinder Camera NEW! | Yes | FBN | $6,900.00 | $6,900.00 | 1 | 2011-02-08 |
| | Leica M9 GREY Full Frame 18mp Rangefinder Camera NEW! | Yes | FBN | $6,900.00 | $6,900.00 | 1 | 2011-01-28 |
| | Leica M9 GREY Full Frame 18mp Rangefinder Camera NEW! | Yes | FBN | $6,900.00 | $6,900.00 | 1 | 2011-02-03 |
| | Leica M9 Rangefinder Digital Camera Body (Grey) 10705 | Yes | FBN | $6,995.00 | $6,900.00 | 1 | 2011-04-23 |
| | NEW Leica M9 Black Full Frame 18mp Camera FREE SHIPPING | Yes | FBN | $6,825.00 | $6,825.00 | 1 | 2011-02-09 |
| | NEW Leica M9 Black Full Frame 18mp Camera Un-Opened Box | Yes | FBN | $6,825.00 | $6,825.00 | 1 | 2011-02-07 |
| | Leica M9 Rangefinder Digital Camera Body (Grey) 10705 | Yes | FBN | $6,995.00 | $6,800.00 | 1 | 2011-04-19 |
| | Leica M9 Steel Gray 18MP Camera Body 10 Condition used | Yes | FBN | $6,722.00 | $6,722.00 | 1 | 2011-03-11 |
| | LEICA M9 STEEL GREY FULL FRAME CAMERA BODY USED-MINT | Yes | 📷 | $6,722.00 | $6,700.00 | 1 | 2011-02-26 |
| | LEICA M9 BLACK PAINT FULL FRAME CAMERA BODY USED-MINT | Yes | 📷 | $6,697.00 | $6,697.00 | 1 | 2011-02-16 |
| | Leica M9 18 Megapixel Digital Camera BLACK PAINT BODY | Yes | Bid | $6,695.00 | $6,695.00 | 2 | 2011-03-02 |
| | Leica M9 Digital 18 MP Camera Performs perfectly Mint! | Yes | 📷 | $6,684.00 | $6,684.00 | 1 | 2011-03-12 |
| | Leica M9 18 Megapixel Digital Camera MINT- | Yes | Bid | $5,916.00 | $6,638.00 | 1 | 2011-03-20 |

We can see at exactly what time of day, day of the week and listing type that the item sold the most for. We also can see what the top of the market is for this item being sold on eBay. Don't be too concerned with the average sale price is when doing a search like this one, as you can see the average price is only $1002, while the top of the sales is just about $7000. This would be a huge discrepancy in price, however what is also included in the search results are accessories for this camera such as lenses, adapters, cases, etc. We can use the same search query and click on the categories on the left to search deeper and more precise. The modified search is pictured on the following page.

As you can see here the results are now confined to only the listings that were in the actual digital cameras category. At the very bottom of the sales results the lowest sales of this camera were for cameras that were sold "for parts or repair" and the ones above those were listed with very poor listing titles that did not attract enough qualified bidders to the listing and sold for less than market value, we will be discussing keyword listing under seller best practices later in this book so for now just understand that a short and keyword lacking title is very bad. So we can narrow our potential resale price in the $6000-$7000 range. This will give us a better idea of how much room we have for profit depending on our purchase price.

Terapeak is a great tool for fast and accurate data on the eBay marketplace, we can also use Amazon to not only find out what the current market value is for used and new books, electronics and an ever expanding marketplace. Searching Amazon will also give us a product description from the manufacturer so we know what should be included with the product when it was purchased new in box.

Personally if I were presented with this situation I would be a buyer up to around $3500 if I just had their word to go by, if I were able to completely test it then perhaps I would pay as much as $5000, anymore and we are not leaving ourselves enough room for market fluctuations, fees and a worthy profit margin.

I understand buying a netbook or laptop with a wireless broadband card and paying a monthly service for internet is not an option for everyone. If you are not interested in that route you can always go to your home, a library, a free wireless hotspot if you have a laptop and do the required research before bidding or buying. Another option, but a rather tedious one as far as I am concerned is using a smartphone to lookup items, if your phone is capable of displaying flash based websites you can access Terapeak. I see a lot of amateur buyers trying to use their cell phones to lookup items in the middle of an auction and they seem to be the same ones making bad purchasing decisions. To be able to make proper comparable searches for an item you need to be looking at multiple listings and sites if possible and doing so on a phone is very time consuming if done correctly as I have tried this many times. In any scenario if you are planning to do research always leave yourself enough time to be able to conduct your due diligence, otherwise you will just be throwing darts at a dartboard until you have a better understanding of resale values. I encounter dealers and resellers all the time that have been in the business their whole lives that I can outbid because I have access to better information and resources using technology. If you cannot find a comparable sale for an item using Terapeak and you have used the 90 day period range throughout the entire year and no information is available on Amazon or using a Google search I recommend passing on the item, especially if you are new to the business because you might end up never selling it and freezing up capital that could be better spent elsewhere.

## What to watch out for

Many times you will be presented with something that seems too good to be true and I hate to write it but yes, it usually is too good to be true. Unfortunately the market is flooded with knock offs and reproductions and the counterfeiters just keep getting better at it. I have been burned several times in my life but it typically happens when I am buying from a category of products I am not very familiar with. Several times I have purchased reproduction antique weapons that someone decided to bury in their backyard for a few years as to add some age and patina to the metal. Spotting fake and reproduction antiques takes a well trained eye and a lot of experience. For instance, if an item you suspect is not antique look to see if it has screws or nails anywhere and if they appear to be hand forged and not made by a machine? Is there a Made in China sticker on the bottom? Ok, let's be a little bit serious here, if you are not sure about the authenticity of an item DO NOT BUY IT! Or find an expert who you can trust to fill in the blanks for you! I am certainly not an antiques appraiser or an expert on general antiques, Victorian period, Renaissance, Middle Ages or Jurassic Period items for that matter. However, what I do possess is an army of antique dealers, collectors, appraisers and experts in just about every field imaginable at my disposal. Just like Henry Ford said, "it's not what you know, it's who you know". I still feel knowledge is true power, but combine street smarts with knowledge and there can be no limits to potential!

Another classic blunder that many newbies make the mistake of doing is trying to by brand named items wholesale. I say mistake because almost always they end up buying knock off inventory from China or another country that turns its back on Trademark infringement and copyrights. If one were to do a search for wholesale NFL jerseys on a wholesale site such as Alibaba they would be provided with many product results from various distributors around the world. Most of which will claim that they are selling authentic jerseys and when you purchase them they will in fact come with NFL stickers and tags, quoting the MSRP value of $249. You only have to pay $20 a jersey and you think this is how business works and wholesaling is a piece of cake. It does not work that way, if you are offered wholesale genuine merchandise for less than 10% of the true value of the item you need to start asking questions. Don't get me wrong, the distributors will send you the jerseys as promised but they will not be created by or for Nike or Adidas or Under Armor but in fact just be creations and copies of the authentic product made in their factories.

Looking for drop shipping and wholesale companies can be a challenge. When searching for such companies it will be hard to find the actual business or distributor offering such an account. You will instead run into loads of companies paying top dollar for search engine placement and rankings for these search terms. You will be offered this great membership that you can sign up and pay a onetime fee of $50 or so and get unlimited access to products you can drop ship or wholesale. NEVER pay to setup a wholesale account or drop shipping account, distributors want you to sell their products and they are not going to charge you a fee to get you to sign up.

This same basic principal can be applied to print ads and radio advertisements about special one day only everything must go everything priced at wholesale rates. These sales are frequently held at convention centers where salesmen and companies rent out booths and tables to push their products. If there is an entry fee to get into the building to purchase merchandise don't be fooled! You will be paying top dollar for products you could find elsewhere. Products will be peddled by high pressure salesmen and the merchandise quality will usually be less than par. The main ploy involved in these types of sales is psychology. The vendors know that you just paid to get into this sale and therefore it is unlikely that you will just leave without purchasing anything. Customers feel as though they are obligated to buy something since they invested their time coming to the sale and had to pay to get in. If nothing else you are going to want to walk around the entire sale and see everything that is offered and end up getting sold by a salesman in a cheap suit. I am not talking about flea markets, you can find some good deals at some of those and you can also negotiate just don't pay to get in!

# Chapter 2 – Marketplaces & Venues

Trying to find the right place to sell an item, service or whatever it may be can be a trying and frustrating experience. If you are looking to sell online there may be a million different websites that will gladly accommodate you and some may even be free to sell on. Just because something is free does not necessarily mean you should use it. I mean let's be realistic if you find one hundred sites that will let you sell products free of charge are you going to spend days listing your products on every site and than if one product actually sells going through and taking the product off of the other 99 sites you listed it on? No! This makes no sense, my advice to you will be to find three or four sites that you are comfortable selling on, pay the fees and make some money. You will want to chose sites that have enough traffic to actually sell your goods, if you are looking for sites other than the most popular ones such as eBay, Amazon, Craigslist, etc you should use sites like alexa.com or compete.com to analyze the amount of traffic a site is actually receiving as well as how long they have been in business.

This chapter will just be more of an overview, so if you are already familiar with one of the sites mentioned you can skim through it. We will be discussing selling strategies and how to sell later in this book.

# The eBay Marketplace

The first place many new sellers think about when they want to sell online is usually eBay and it is a great place to get your feet wet but it should not be an end all selling platform. eBay was founded way back in 1995 and started out as just a small online auction site whose focus was on collectibles. Some of the most popular early sales were those of Pez dispensers but since eBay's humble beginnings it has grown into a massive conglomerate of online sales sites. Some of their popular sites include eBay.com, PayPal.com, Half.com, Rent.com, Shopping.com, Stubhub.com, Skype.com, StumbleUpon.com, Kijiji.com just to name a few of the most popular ones. The total assets reported in 2010 were over 22 billion dollars and eBay is a publically traded company so you don't have to worry about them stealing your credit card and disappearing in the middle of the night.

The main eBay.com site is what we will be focusing on first; There are four different types of selling formats that we will be using; Online Auction, eBay Store/Fixed Price Listings, eBay Motors and eBay Classifieds. The first type of selling that will be discussed is online auctions. In order to sell on eBay you will first need to create an eBay user account which is completely free. After you have created a user account on eBay you will need to upgrade to a seller account, which is also free but you will be required to input your billing information. Now that you are a seller on eBay, you will have the option of listing items for online auction with listing durations of 1,3,5,7 and 10 days. eBay has just launched FREE LISTINGS! Pay no insertion fees on your first 50 items EVERY MONTH! That is new as of September, 2011 and I have never seen them do anything like this before. They are really trying to bring more sellers out of the dark. If you happen to go over your 50 listings, the following insertion fees apply for auction listings:

## Insertion fees for auction-style format listings

### Auction-style format listings

| Starting or reserve price | | Insertion fee |
|---|---|---|
| $0.01–$0.99 | | $0.10 |
| $1.00–$9.99 | | $0.25 |
| $10.00–$24.99 | Free for 50 listings per month | $0.50 |
| $25.00–$49.99 | | $0.75 |
| $50.00–$199.99 | | $1.00 |
| $200.00 or more | | $2.00 |

When an auction ends and the item sells there is a final value fee that is added to the cost of selling the item. That provides eBay with more incentives to promote your products and drive traffic to the listings, the higher the item sells the more money they will make and you will make!

In late 2011 eBay decided that eBay sellers were dodging and avoiding higher final value fees by charging outrageous shipping cost and selling items very low. This allowed sellers to per say sell an item for a dollar and charge $20 for shipping making the total cost to the buyer $21. The seller would realistically only be paying a fraction of the shipping charge to ship out the item and rely on playing on the buyers mindset that they are getting a great deal for an item and not considering the actual cost of shipping said merchandise to them. In such cases the seller would only have to pay a very minimal final value fee based on the $1 sale and no charge on the shipping fee allowing sellers to add in profits. This was also beneficial in listing items, they could pay just ten cents to list that item instead of paying twenty five cents to list it for a higher starting price but achieve the same gross revenue from the sale. Eventually eBay caught on and decided to charge final value fees based on the total price of an item which included the shipping and handling charge. As of 2012 the final value fee is calculated as follows:

## Final value fees for auction-style format listings

| Auction-style format listings | |
|---|---|
| Total cost to buyer (less any sales tax) | Final value fee (Based on the total amount of the sale, including the cost of the item, shipping, and any other fees a seller may charge, excluding any sales tax) |
| Item not sold | No fee |
| $0.01–$50.00 | 9.0% of the item's total cost to buyer with a maximum charge of $100.00. |
| $50.01–$1,000.00 | |
| $1,000.01 or more | |

The next selling format that we will use is known as fixed price listing, and this can be used with or without an eBay store. Please note that if you do sign up for an eBay store you will no longer be eligible for the 50 free auction style insertion fees per month. On the flip side of that, if you have a store you will be eligible for discounted fixed priced listing fees. If you decide not to sign-up for a store at first the following insertion fee applies for each fixed priced listing you submit:

If you are a low volume seller, or you are just getting started than use the 50 free auction listings and get your feet wet with some sales experience and then consider upgrading to more advanced features. eBay store discounted fixed price fees and monthly cost of each membership level are as follows:

| Fees | Basic Store | Premium Store | Anchor Store |
|---|---|---|---|
| Monthly subscription | $15.95 | $49.95 | $299.95 |
| Discounted Fixed Price Insertion Fee | 20¢ | 5¢ | 3¢ |

When you sell a fixed price item final value fees will be applied just as they are with online auction style listings however the breakdown is slightly different and the total fees range between seven to thirteen percent of the total value.

There are many upgrades and listing enhancements available to sellers when listing in both auction and fixed price format. The first one that many sellers consider is setting a reserve price, especially when an item is of great value and they are worried about selling an item at too low a sales price. The reserve price is only for online auctions and the cost is as follows:

▼Reserve price fees

| Reserve price | Fee |
|---|---|
| $0.01 - $199.99 | **$2.00** |
| $200.00 and up | **1.0% of reserve price (up to $50.00)** |

Generally seasoned sellers do not use reserve prices when listing auctions as the fee will greatly eat into your profits if you list many items with reserve prices and they do not sell. If you have an item that you don't want to sell for less than say $100 it would be a better strategy to list the item as a fixed price listing for that amount or a higher, or start the item out in an auction style format at $99.99. Reserve price listings have been greatly phased out from most auctions that you will encounter. Another cost effective strategy that is somewhat of a gray area with sellers is to list items starting out at .99 cents and then ending the listing on eBay if their desired price is not reached by the last day of auction. You can end any eBay listing, even if it has bids as long as there are more than 12 hours left. I do not recommend making this a common practice but the option is out there for you.

There is another upgrade that is offered that you can apply to your auction style listings to give them the same feel as a fixed price listing which is a buy it now price. This upgrade is great for items that will have a lot of potential bidders and if there is a bidding war for your item, potential buyers may just pay a little bit more and use your buy it now feature, to ensure that they will win the item. Fees for buy it now:

| Buy It Now price* | Fee | |
|---|---|---|
| $0.99 - $9.99 | | $0.05 |
| $10.00 - $24.99 | Free for 50 listings per month | $0.10 |
| $25.00 - $49.99 | | $0.20 |
| $50.00 or more | | $0.25 |

There are some upgrades that I refuse to waste my money on, one of the popular listing upgrades that many sellers without much technical knowledge waste their money on is the eBay picture hosting fees. Basically if you have six pictures of your item that you want displayed on your listing and you do not

know anything about HTML which is the web language that eBay listings can use than you might have to pay these fees:
▼ **eBay picture hosting fees**

| Feature | Fee |
| --- | --- |
| First picture | Free |
| Each additional picture | $0.15 |
| **Picture Pack** (1-6 pictures) | $0.75 |
| **Picture Pack** (7-12 pictures) | $1.00 |

A simple solution to this problem of paying eBay to host your pictures is to sign-up with a Godaddy.com hosting account, you can get one setup and pay less than $5 a month for it. This will allow you to upload all of your pictures to your hosting account and display them within your listing free of charge. There are several FREE eBay listing templates in your members section that can be edited to display your own pictures through your hosting account. There is an instructional video also in our video section with step by step instructions on how to complete this procedure.

I recommend always using the gallery upgrade option on your listings, this used to have a fee of .25 cents per listing but has now been changed to free. This provides your auction listing with a small thumbnail picture that can be seen in the standard search results. I will also use the option of listing in two categories on occasion. This upgrade doubles all of your fees and is best used when your insertion fee is at a minimum but you expect the final sales price to be high enough to justify it. For example, if I list an item at auction starting out at .99 cents with no other upgrades my insertion fee is only .10

cents. If I wanted my item to have more exposure and there was another relevant category for my item I could chose to list it in both categories and my total insertion fee would be .20 cents. I tend to use this upgrade when an item I have is either not very popular and I need to attract as many bidders as possible to get a potential sale, or there are two separate relevant categories for my listing and I feel that the item is worth at least $50. Subtitle can also be useful if you cannot fit all of the keywords and basic description you want into your eBay title. The keywords used in the subtitle are not searchable so don't waste the subtitle description with useless keywords but instead put something there that will stand out and entice a potential buyer to click your listing instead of another one. This will also help your listing stand out on the eBay search page, as will using the Bold upgrade, but Bold is rather costly and should only be done with items of greater value. The listing designer upgrade is a visual enhancement template that eBay provides and it is free if you are subscribed to eBay seller manager pro. The basic listing upgrade fees for auctions and fixed price listings are as follows:

▼Listing upgrade fees

| Feature | Fee - auction-style and fixed price format (3, 5, 7, 10 Days) | Fee - fixed price format (30 Days, Good 'Til Cancelled) |
| --- | --- | --- |
| **Value Pack** | $0.65 | $2.00 |
| **Gallery** | Free | Free |
| **Gallery Plus** | $0.35 | $1.00 |
| **Listing** | $0.10 | $0.30 |

| | | |
|---|---|---|
| **Designer*** | | |
| **Subtitle**** | $0.50 | $1.50 |
| **Bold** | $2.00 | $4.00 |
| **Scheduled listings** | $0.10 | $0.10 |
| **List in 2 categories** | Insertion and listing upgrade fees are doubled.<br><br>Scheduled listing and final value fees are charged once. | Insertion and listing upgrade fees are doubled.<br><br>Scheduled listing and final value fees are charged once. |

There are several tools and services that eBay provides to sellers to help them facilitate and automate the listing and sales process. Turbo Lister is a free tool that I recommend you download right now if you have not yet done so.

▼**Seller tool fees**

| Seller tool | Fee |
|---|---|

| Turbo Lister | Free |
|---|---|
| Selling Manager | Free |
| Selling Manager Pro* | $15.99 per month |
| Blackthorne Basic **(Free 30-day trial)** | $9.99 per month |
| Blackthorne Pro **(Free 30-day trial)*** | $24.99 per month |
|  |  |

The third type of listing format we will be using will be eBay Motors, I have not utilized this format for sometime but it is still an effective means of selling automotive vehicles. To date I have sold eleven cars on eBay Motors, a $280,000 RV, a Jet ski and a few motorcycles. The fees are as follows:

| Vehicles: Fees on the first 4 listings in a 12-month period * | | | |
|---|---|---|---|
| **Category** | **Insertion fee** | **Successful listing fee** | |
|  |  | Final bid amount: $2000 or less | Final bid amount: $2000.01 or more |

| | | | |
|---|---|---|---|
| Cars & Trucks, RVs & Campers, and Commercial Trucks | $0.00 | $60.00 | $125.00 |
| Motorcycles, Powersports, Trailers and Boats | $0.00 | $60.00 | $125.00 |
| Powersports under 50cc | $0.00 | $10.00 | $10.00 |
| All other vehicles | $0.00 | $60.00 | $125.00 |

*A 12-month period starts on the day you first submit a listing and ends 12 months later

**Vehicles: Fees starting with the 5th listing in a 12-month period***

| Category | Insertion fee | Successful listing fee | |
|---|---|---|---|
| | | Final bid amount: $5000 or less | Final bid amount: $5000.01 or more |

| | | | |
|---|---|---|---|
| Cars & Trucks, RVs & Campers, and Commercial Trucks | $50.00 | $0.00 | $0.00 |
| Motorcycles, Powersports, Trailers and Boats | $20.00 | $30.00 | $60.00 |
| Powersports under 50cc | $10.00 | $10.00 | $10.00 |
| All other vehicles | $20.00 | $30.00 | $60.00 |

The last sales format we will use is the eBay Classified Ad type. This feature will have its uses for us but I will get into that a bit later as it can be used to sell Businesses, Websites, Timeshares, Household goods and a lot more types of items.

**Classified Ad listing type**

| Duration | Insertion fee |
|---|---|
| 30-day listing for most categories: | $9.95 |

As a seller you will want to pay attention to eBay's fees as they change frequently, for instance a few years ago sellers could list as many items as they wanted at whatever price they wanted in their eBay store for one cent per listing. As a result of this eBay became flooded with sellers listing thousands of the same products and there was not enough buyers to keep up with the products being listed and selling was very difficult. To compensate and try and balance out the marketplace eBay raised fees to a maximum of 20 cents per listing to force sellers to list less products and therefore buyers had less choices to chose from and sellers have had a much stronger sales result as a whole. This type of trend has existed on eBay since their inception with the constant change in fees to try and keep a balanced marketplace so buyers and sellers can benefit.

Selling on eBay can be a very rewarding option but there are some drawbacks to the site. Over the years eBay has enforced a growing number of policies to restrict the power that sellers on the site have. They have implemented a buyer protection policy that most buyers are eligible for which requires sellers to ship only to the verified address of a buyer. It provides buyers the opportunity to buy without worry, if they are not satisfied with the item or for virtually any other reason they can return the item to the seller and receive a full refund, including original shipping. Sellers have virtually no say in the matter, even if in the listing description the buyer states that they do not allow returns, or that only the sales price not shipping is refunded eBay will trump that and freeze the money in your PayPal account until the matter is resolved. PayPal has become virtually the only payment method accepted on eBay, with good reason because eBay acquired PayPal and has built their business model around it. Money orders, checks, even business checks are no longer allowed to be advertised as acceptable payment methods, with the exception of cash on pickup. I can remember in the beginning days of my eBay sales I would receive envelopes with cash and checks daily, now I can't remember the last time I got one. If a buyer asks you directly if you will accept cash or a check than you are allowed to accept it if you chose to do so but you cannot put in your listing description that you will. There are also some other small payment processers that eBay allows, the list of approved ones can be found on their site.

The DSR system has been implemented for sellers which is a detailed seller report system in which buyers leave feedback for the transaction but can also leave anywhere from one to five stars for a seller under specific aspects of the transaction such as shipping and handling prices, communication, item as described. If a seller receives to many low ratings in any category they will be penalized or even suspended from selling. On the flip side of that if a seller receives an average of 4.8 stars per transaction with less than .05% of buyers leaving a one or two star rating for a transaction than they will be considered a "Top Rated Seller" and receive 20% off of their final value fees as well as higher placement in search results on the site. If a sellers DSR starts dropping it will greatly reduce the success a seller will have, for one thing the items they are listing on the site will be harder for buyers to find as eBay will place higher rated sellers listings above lower ones by default.

Sellers opening accounts after 2010 by default will have restrictions on the amount of items that they can list per month and the amount of total sales value that they can do per month, the total sales also includes items that you currently have listed in your store and for auction so even if you have not sold anything in the current month but you have $5000 worth of inventory listed in your store you may not be able to list anymore items that month. In order to lift the restrictions sellers have to prove that they can meet eBay's requirements and after about six months they will raise the limits. The other methods of raising or removing limits is to contact eBay and talk to one of their representatives and plead your case for removing limits, or if you have an established eBay account prior to 2010 that is in good standing you can link your new account to that one and lift the limits.

eBay will also use PayPal to hold any new sellers payments for a period of 30 days after they have been received or until a buyer leaves positive feedback for the transaction which can be a huge pain for new sellers trying to flip inventory on a low budget.

eBay has also greatly increased the number and types of items and services that cannot be listed on their site. Here is a list of prohibited items:

- Adult Only category
- alcohol (see also wine)
- animals and wildlife products – examples include live animals, mounted specimens, and ivory
- art
- artifacts, grave-related items, and Native American arts and crafts
- catalytic converters and test pipes
- cell phone (wireless) service contracts
- charity or fundraising listings
- clothing, used
- contracts
- cosmetics, used
- counterfeit currency and stamps
- credit cards
- currency, selling
- drugs and drug paraphernalia
- drugs, describing drugs or drug-like substances
- electronics equipment – examples include cable TV de-scramblers, radar scanners, and traffic signal control devices
- electronic surveillance equipment – examples include wiretapping devices and telephone bugging devices
- embargoed goods and prohibited countries – examples include items from Cuba
- event tickets
- firearms, weapons, and knives – examples include pepper spray, replicas, and stun guns (see also military items)
- food and healthcare items
- gift cards

- government documents, IDs, and licenses
- government, transit, and shipping-related items – examples include airplane operations manuals, subway employee uniforms, and U.S. Postal Service (USPS) mailbags
- hazardous materials – examples include batteries, fireworks, and refrigerants
- human parts and remains
- importation of goods into the United States – examples include CDs that were intended only for distribution in a certain country
- international trading
- items encouraging illegal activity – examples include an eBook describing how to create methamphetamine
- lockpicking devices
- lottery tickets
- mailing lists and personal information
- manufacturers' coupons
- medical devices – examples include contact lenses, pacemakers, and surgical instruments
- military items (see also firearms, weapons, and knives)
- multi-level marketing, pyramid, and matrix programs
- offensive material – examples include ethnically or racially offensive material and Nazi memorabilia
- pesticides
- plants and seeds
- police-related items
- political memorabilia (reproduction)
- postage meters
- prescription drugs
- prohibited services
- real estate
- recalled items
- slot machines
- stamps
- stocks and other securities
- stolen property and property with removed serial numbers
- surveillance equipment

- tobacco
- travel
- weeds (see plants and seeds)

I will discuss how to effectively sell on eBay later in this book under how to sell. For now you should just understand that you can sell just about anything on eBay that does not fit into the banned categories listed above. eBay will be one of our biggest resources for quick sales and flipping as well as buying opportunities.

# Selling on Amazon

Amazon has quickly become a seller's best friend! It has surpassed eBay.com in daily traffic according to Alexa.com which is a top web information company (ironically owned by Amazon). Amazon is currently ranked #5 most visited site in the US by traffic rank and eBay.com is ranked #9 as of June, 2011. However globally both eBay and Amazon have their own domain names for each country they provide service too so total traffic still favors eBay when we take into account those international sites. Regardless, Amazon being the highest ranked E-Commerce site in the United States means big money for United States sellers.

Amazon has been a leader in E-Commerce since the dawn of internet commerce. They gained a reputation early as being the one stop shop to buy books, and many people today still think of Amazon as a book marketplace. Amazon is so much more than a book vendor, basically any item that has a UPC number or an ISBN can be sold by us sellers on their platform. The sales prices are generally higher than on eBay and much less competition with items such as electronics, cell phones, computers and even instruments. Best of all, there are no fees for listing on Amazon! You can have five thousand books and electronics listed on Amazon without paying a cent! This translates into slightly higher final value fees for low cost items so don't waste your time with items that will only sell for a few dollars. As sellers on Amazon we lose the right to calculate the shipping cost to our customers who buy from us and instead Amazon uses their own shipping calculator and fixed shipping fees.

The Amazon seller marketplace has a very different sales model for sellers. Instead of buyers bidding up on items against other buyers sellers bid down to get the lowest price against other sellers of an item. What this means is that essentially sellers bid against other sellers for pricing.

Amazon does not work like the eBay marketplace for payments, payments for all items that are sold on their site are processed by Amazon and dispersed every two weeks to the sellers bank account.

There are two main types of direct Amazon seller accounts; the first type is the basic and free to list and no monthly fees account. The next type of account is the PRO Merchant account and the third type is an Amazon Fulfillment (FBA) program. I usually switch back and forth from PRO Merchant to Basic seller account depending on how much inventory I am selling on average in a month or if I get a load of books in. The quick low down with the PRO Merchant account is that there is a $39.99 fee per month, and with this fee it allows sellers to save $.99 in fees per item sold during the month. If you sell 43 items in a month and you don't have a PRO Merchant account you would have paid an extra few dollars in fees and the PRO Merchant account would have benefited you. There are also additional features of the upgrade, below are snap shots of my account upgraded as a PRO Merchant and the fees as well as a featured menu with added options:

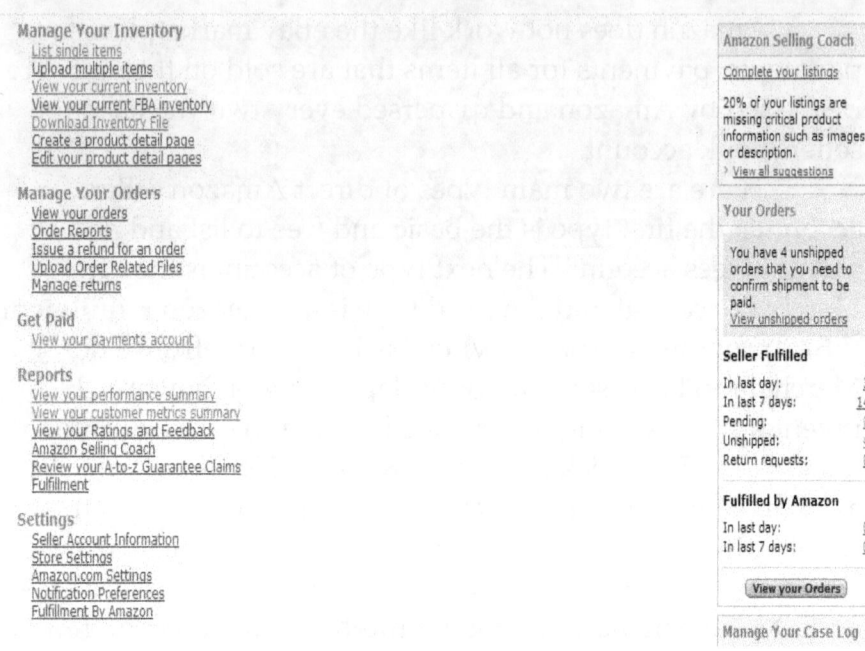

In the above shot my PRO account has the option to Upload multiple Items, Download my Inventory to a spreadsheet file, Create and Edit my own product detail pages which means I can create new listings on Amazon which basic members cannot. I also have access to the Amazon Selling Coach and various other tools. The first snap shot below is of my account as a basic member and the fee breakdown; the second is of my account as a PRO Merchant.

| Transaction type | Order ID | Product Details | Total product charges | Total promotional rebates | Amazon fees | Other | Total |
|---|---|---|---|---|---|---|---|
| Other | --- | Shipping services | $0.00 | $0.00 | $0.00 | $-5.65 | $-5.65 |
| Order Payment | 103-7244345-9470667 | Blue Samsung Exclaim M550 for Sprint | $44.99 | $0.00 | $-5.04 | $4.49 | $44.44 |
| Other | --- | Shipping services | $0.00 | $0.00 | $0.00 | $-2.31 | $-2.31 |
| Order Payment | 002-6571795-0670617 | The Judas Window | $9.79 | $0.00 | $-3.81 | $3.99 | $9.97 |
| Order Payment | 105-2675342-9455403 | Ramset Powder Fastening Systems TF1100 T... | $349.99 | $0.00 | $-44.29 | $12.99 | $318.69 |
| Other | --- | Shipping services | $0.00 | $0.00 | $0.00 | $-2.48 | $-2.48 |
| Order Payment | 002-4179199-2439447 | Illustrated Course Guide: Microsoft Offi... | $9.66 | $0.00 | $-3.79 | $3.99 | $9.86 |
| Other | --- | Shipping services | $0.00 | $0.00 | $0.00 | $-2.89 | $-2.89 |
| Order Payment | 102-7700939-5617066 | The Day of St. Anthony's Fire | $8.66 | $0.00 | $-3.64 | $3.99 | $9.01 |
| Other | --- | Shipping services | $0.00 | $0.00 | $0.00 | $-2.89 | $-2.89 |
| Order Payment | 002-5042112-7951426 | A Little Maid of New Orleans | $10.77 | $0.00 | $-3.96 | $3.99 | $10.80 |
| Other | --- | Shipping services | $0.00 | $0.00 | $0.00 | $-2.89 | $-2.89 |
| Order Payment | 103-1619680-5829023 | The Boy With A Drum, A Little Golden Boo... | $9.99 | $0.00 | $-3.84 | $3.99 | $10.14 |
| Refund | 105-0402189-9005033 | Sony MDSJE320 MiniDisc Recorder | $-149.99 | $0.00 | $14.53 | $-15.40 | $-150.86 |
| Other | --- | Shipping services | $0.00 | $0.00 | $0.00 | $-3.71 | $-3.71 |
| Order Payment | 103-7595920-2936256 | Complete Illustrated Thorburn's Mammals | $12.77 | $0.00 | $-4.26 | $3.99 | $12.50 |
| Order Payment | 103-0844913-8130663 | AT&T Bogen Friday FR-2000 Two-Line Digi... | $199.99 | $0.00 | $-17.69 | $6.99 | $189.29 |

And then the PRO Merchant billing…from a few days after I upgraded….

| Transaction type | Order ID | Product Details | Total product charges | Total promotional rebates | Amazon fees | Other | Total |
|---|---|---|---|---|---|---|---|
| Order Payment | 103-8736847-7511408 | Canon PIXMA mini260 Photo Inkjet Printer... | $69.99 | $0.00 | $-8.03 | $14.41 | $76.37 |
| Shipping Services | 104-4573844-0406654 | Billing | $-3.01 | $0.00 | $-0.07 | $0.00 | $-3.08 |
| Order Payment | 104-4573844-0406654 | Let's Make Noise: At the Airport | $5.66 | $0.00 | $-3.19 | $3.99 | $6.46 |
| Shipping Services | 103-6401934-1319460 | Billing | $-13.46 | $0.00 | $-0.07 | $0.00 | $-13.53 |
| Order Payment | 103-6401934-1319460 | JVC HRJ692U 4-Head Hi-Fi VCR , Black | $59.99 | $0.00 | $-6.89 | $10.99 | $64.09 |
| Shipping Services | 105-2355505-2591415 | Billing | $-36.04 | $0.00 | $-0.07 | $0.00 | $-36.11 |
| Order Payment | 105-2355505-2591415 | Dell LP1700N Network Laser Printer (25pp... | $129.99 | $0.00 | $-13.24 | $18.49 | $135.24 |
| Shipping Services | 103-8009982-0221806 | Billing | $-4.05 | $0.00 | $-0.07 | $0.00 | $-4.12 |
| Order Payment | 103-8009982-0221806 | Adventures in English Literature: Grade ... | $19.99 | $0.00 | $-5.34 | $3.99 | $18.64 |
| Shipping Services | 002-6629378-1892211 | Billing | $-2.82 | $0.00 | $-0.07 | $0.00 | $-2.89 |
| Order Payment | 002-6629378-1892211 | The Book of Jewish Practice | $13.88 | $0.00 | $-4.42 | $3.99 | $13.45 |
| Shipping Services | 102-0361532-0203419 | Billing | $-4.05 | $0.00 | $-0.07 | $0.00 | $-4.12 |
| Order Payment | 102-0361532-0203419 | Adobe Photoshop CS3 for Photographers: A... | $10.22 | $0.00 | $-3.87 | $3.99 | $10.34 |
| Order Payment | 102-9739187-1858668 | Canon PIXMA MP500 All-In-One Photo Print... | $99.99 | $0.00 | $-10.89 | $18.99 | $108.09 |
| Shipping Services | 002-0824880-7640230 | Billing | $-3.64 | $0.00 | $-0.07 | $0.00 | $-3.71 |
| Order Payment | 002-0824880-7640230 | Hieronymous Bosch (Library of Great Pain... | $39.99 | $0.00 | $-8.34 | $3.99 | $35.64 |
| Shipping Services | 102-7358798-0426644 | Billing | $-3.64 | $0.00 | $-0.07 | $0.00 | $-3.71 |
| Order Payment | 102-7358798-0426644 | Who's Who in Rock & Roll | $9.99 | $0.00 | $-3.84 | $3.99 | $10.14 |

Incase you were wondering, the billing charges are for shipping, you don't pay for shipping out of your own pocket. The customer pays Amazon a total amount and you pay for shipping charges out of that amount which is great because you don't have to put money up front if you are shipping massive amounts of items and than waiting to be paid. The issue with the current shipping system that Amazon has setup is that it is only good for USPS, but it will do all available services such as International First Class, Media Mail but if you need to ship with UPS or FedEx you will have to front the money for shipping.

If you don't want to worry about shipping out items and maintaining inventory there is another solution. It is called the Amazon fulfillment program. This program is very simple and can save you a lot of time but may drastically kill your profits. With this program you are basically merging your inventory with Amazon's inventory which raises your sell through rate and your product is shown before sellers listing new and used items. Also if you're using the multi-channel fulfillment option Amazon will use 3rd party sites and affiliates to help sell your products for an extra fee per sale. There are several fees associated with this program and guidelines; here is a snapshot of some of the fees:

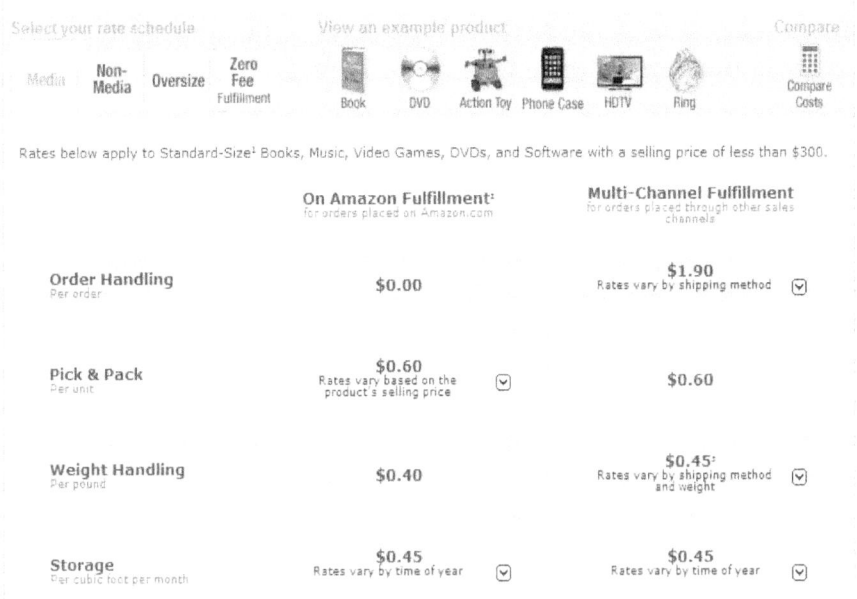

Rates below apply to Standard-Size[1] Books, Music, Video Games, DVDs, and Software with a selling price of less than $300.

|  | On Amazon Fulfillment[1] for orders placed on Amazon.com | Multi-Channel Fulfillment for orders placed through other sales channels |
|---|---|---|
| **Order Handling** Per order | $0.00 | $1.90 Rates vary by shipping method |
| **Pick & Pack** Per unit | $0.60 Rates vary based on the product's selling price | $0.60 |
| **Weight Handling** Per pound | $0.40 | $0.45[1] Rates vary by shipping method and weight |
| **Storage** Per cubic foot per month | $0.45 Rates vary by time of year | $0.45 Rates vary by time of year |

If you are interested in their fulfillment program you login to your seller account and click on fulfillment account under the seller menu. Once you have enrolled in this program you can choose which books you want to include, you type in an ISBN or UPC number and Amazon lets you know what the current market price of the item is and you chose the price you want the product to sell for and Amazon will display your exact cost/fee breakdown and your net earnings for that particular item. Once you have chosen the products you are happy with and your potential earnings you have to package up all your items and pay for shipping to mail the items to Amazon. You will print out a shipping label through Amazon and a packaging slip to include in the shipment, the next step is just taking it to the post office or having a carrier pickup. I recommend if you are using this service that you pick out books that are not all heavy and have a sales price of at least $20 to make it worth your time because you now will have many additional fees associated with your items including the cost of sending the package(s) to Amazon.

If you understand the risk and rewards associated with this and you don't have time to deal with shipping than this is the program for you!

## Selling on ETSY.COM

This is an up and coming online sales powerhouse that provides sellers of handmade merchandise an opportunity to sell their products and create and promote their brand. ETSY is a marketplace that connects sellers with buyers of artistic products. It has a very special sense of community and really strives to make the experience personable. Since this is a niche marketplace; there are only three types of items that can be sold on this venue. Products that can be sold on ETSY.com include handmade products that are created only by you, supplies for commercial and home use and lastly vintage products that are 20 years or older. So the products that are prohibited from being sold on the site are any that do not fit into the three categories listed.

What can you sell?

Handmade items by you.

Vintage items which are 20 years or older.

Supplies:
Commercial and handmade supplies.

Not allowed
Anything that doesn't fit in one of the three categories.

Handmade goods created by someone else.

Illegal or prohibited items.

How does it work?

You list the item on Etsy for a fee.

Get paid
Shoppers find your item and pay you directly.

You ship the item to your customer.

The ETSY marketplace has come on strong, sellers and buyers are very loyal to the brand. There is no referral or affiliate program but both buyers and sellers have been referring people here as if they were being paid. If this site was not exploding I would not bother telling you about it if you have not already tried it out for yourself, just check out their traffic stats for the last year:

Traffic has more than tripled its traffic in less than a year's time! It has made its way into the top 200 sites in the world and still climbing, this graph shows the level out but

Christmas shopping will sky rocket the site even higher.

Ok, so your saying what is it going to cost me to sell on a somewhat exclusive marketplace. To list an item on ETSY it costs 20 cents but you get triple the listing duration of an eBay listing for your fixed price listings, that's right your item(s) will be listed for 120 days in your ETSY shop. You can list a single type of item with a quantity of 3 and you would pay 60 cents. When your item sells you will be charged a 3.5% commission of the sale price, compare that to eBay's 9% final value fee! Don't get me wrong I am not trying to hate on eBay, I simply want people to open their eyes and see that there may be other options for your online sales. Something else of note is that the user name that you choose to sign up with for your account will also be your store name, so if you pick dan9211 than your store will be http://dan9211.etsy.com – just something to keep in mind.

ETSY sellers can accept PayPal, Credit Cards and Money Orders for payment. Signing up for your ETSY account is free, however it will require a credit card on file to create a seller account and you will be charged a $1 fee just to verify that your card is active. Once your account has been established you can use PayPal as a payment method for your fees as long as you have a valid credit card on file.

If your thinking you have nothing to sell on this site, you may have an epiphany when I show you some simple things you can make in your spare time or have someone make for you and sell for huge profits on ETSY. I will go over what types of products to sell and how to make them later on, for now just keep the ETSY name in the back of your mind.

# Print on Demand - Zazzle – It's just fun to say!

Zazzle.com is more than just a fun name to say, it can do wonders for your bottom line! If you have not done so yet, sign up for a free Zazzle.com account. It is completely free to make an account. Zazzle is definitely a leader in the game of create and print on demand products, t-shirts, mugs, art, wall accessories, electronic device accessories, cards and postage. However, their main competitor whom you may have heard of **Café Press** has been on their heels and both sites still managing to flourish. If this type of marketplace is one that you are interested in pursuing sales on than consider them both interchangeable.

## Why Choose Zazzle?

| | |
|---|---|
| Cost to set up a Store | FREE |
| Number of Monthly Visitors | 20,000,000+ |
| Royalty Rate | Set your own |
| Volume Bonus | Starts at just $100 |
| Additional Earning Potential | 15-30% |
| Refer Any Product on Zazzle | Yes |
| # of Customizable Products | 350+ |
| 100% Customizable Stores | Yes |
| Maximum # of Products Per Store | Unlimited |
| Promotion Tips and Strategies | FREE |

## Classified Postings

By now you have heard of Craigslist and eBay classifieds and maybe Kijiji which is also an eBay company but you may not be aware of the true potential they offer us. You may not be aware of the sheer amount of classified ad sites available to us online and how to fully use their features. Classified ad sites are usually free for most postings which alone is a huge draw to use them. I like to think of classified sites as the trifecta of marketplaces, they provide us a means to sell virtually anything online, they provide us a way to buy inventory for resale and finally they allow us to build a network of potential buyers, partners and coops.

Do a search on Google, Bing and Yahoo for "free classifieds" and "classifieds" and make a list of five to ten of the top classified ad sites, or make a bookmark folder of them because you will need them later on. I can't stress enough that you need to use different search engines when trying to find classified sites. Each search engine will display various top results as the ranking metrics vary for each search engine.

I will get into specific listing techniques, what to list and buy and how to properly use the power of classified sites later on in this book so for now just take a few minutes to sign up for Craigslist and a few other sites and familiarize yourself with those sites so you are ready when it is time to use them.

## Forums & Blogs?

There are no specific forums or blogs that I am going to go over, the use of forums and blogs will be more geared to niche sales and leads. If you already have products you want to sell, a service or genre you are interested in you can spend some time right now and build a list of potential sites. They will provide us the ability to reach a niche customer base related to your market.

Let's say for instance that you own a Corvette and this is your absolute passion and you are interested in selling something related to Corvettes. Go ahead and pull up Google, Bing and Yahoo and do some searches for "Corvette forum" "Corvette Blog" "Chevy Forum" "Chevy Blog" "Automotive Forums" and other similar queries. Make a list of as many relevant forums and blogs that you can locate and if you have time go ahead and sign-up for these blogs and forums. If you sign-up now, go ahead and make some posts or comments on the forum or blog. Make them friendly, answer a question somebody has posted that needs an answer, introduce yourself, etc. The point of doing this is to start a positive reputation and add some age to your account. This way your rating will go up, credibility and you won't run the risk of being banned as a spammer later on if you are trying to sell products. We won't be spamming, but some sites and moderators will kill threads and postings from new members making their first posts. Blogs and forums certainly may be a way for you to successfully market, promote and sell effectively. One of the key features to most of these venues is that they are almost always free to sign up and list your products on. The downside is simply that it is hard to sell in volume this way because you have to answer a lot of e-mails and direct selling, unlike selling on auto-pilot elsewhere.

## Selling Offline

For those of you willing to get off the couch for a little while and get out into the world for a bit you may find it rewarding. Selling online does have the benefits of convenience, everything is a few clicks away on your computer and when you get paid the money can be sent right to your bank account. The added benefit of not having to have customers come to your house to pick up products or having to answer and make phone calls to arrange such a sale keep many people away from doing business offline.

All sales done offline do not have to be done in such a manor though; you can use other companies and salesmen to sell products for you. This type of selling can actually free up the majority of your time and allow you to automate most of your selling. This is a perfect way to start selling if you don't have much free time or if you don't feel like selling online. Personally I know many individuals and dealers that frequent storage auctions and estate auctions and so forth that do not sell online at all. They have proven to me time and again that certain items will draw much higher sales prices by selling locally. Selling items without having to ship them out and pay selling fees for online services can add extra money to your bottom line and increase profits.

The auction flipper is one type of reseller that can act like a foreclosure real estate home flipper. This type of seller never actually has to sell products directly to customers or buy from them. They buy from lower level estate auctions and consignment auctions that sell table lots and boxed lots. This enables them to purchase large quantities of items at a very low price because the auction house is simply liquidating estate inventory and consignment inventory. The reseller than sorts through the inventory they purchased at the lower level auctions and looks for items that can be fixed up, cleaned off or grouped together. For example they may purchase twenty clocks that are in rough shape, but only pay a fraction of their restored or working condition price. Either they do the repairs themselves or have a contact or relationship with someone who can fix them up. They may also purchase various types of items at the sale, for instance sports memorabilia, cameras or paintings. This may be their niche if you will and they will store up these types of items at their house or warehouse.

The flip comes when the reseller locates a specialty auction. Frequently auction houses will have special sit down and premium auctions featuring one type of item for sale or a theme. Say it's a sports memorabilia auction only; they put all of their sports collectibles in the auction on consignment to be resold. The benefit here is that the auction is going to draw sports collectors and the auction house is going to advertise locally to every sports collector they know or can reach to come to this auction and buy sports collectibles. Therefore the reseller will be able to sell the same products that were purchased at the estate or consignment auction at a much higher price because the individual collectors looking for sports memorabilia wouldn't have been at the estate auction which was selling random merchandise.

The reseller or auction flipper may also be able to pull out individual items that are of high value that they purchased in bulk lots at the estate sale or consignment auction. They can put those higher quality and more valuable items into a more prestigious sit down auction houses and high end auctions. As a reseller these would be the types of auctions you would avoid buying items to resell as most of the bidders would be collectors and paying retail or above for rare and valuable collectibles. I have heard stories from dealers I talk with routinely who have found things at the smaller estate auctions and resold them at prestigious auction houses such as Sotheby's and Christies for hundreds of thousands of dollars. To be able to pull off auction flipping requires experience, knowledge and patience. One must first frequent many different auction houses and types of auctions to get an understanding of the types of products usually sold there and the average prices usually paid by the customers who buy there. You must also be able to decipher between reproductions and fakes as well as be able to spot rare collectibles and know what the premium resale value is, not the online price. You must also learn whether products are complete and know if something missing. Instead of relying on eBay online market research tools per say you may want to purchase some collectible price guides that have a massive index with pictures and descriptions of rare collectibles that have sold at public auction before and at high end auctions. These types of rare and unusual items will be hard to find online for comparable sales values so studying these types of books and guides can give you the knowledge you need to find that rare gem hidden in a sea of routine collectibles at an estate auction.

At the auction flippers disposal will not only be other auctions as that may greatly limit the amount of items that can be purchased and types of items. The auction flipper will have a list of antique stores and dealers that will purchase items directly or allow for consignment sales of items in their premium retail stores. The flipper will also sell items to pawn stores and second hand shops. Second hand shops may include sports trading card shops, music stores and dealers and other store fronts that sell used and collectible goods.

Auction flippers are not limited to just estate and consignment auctions, for instance most storage auction buyers will follow the same methods for liquidating their storage units. When buying many storage units the flipper will have mass amounts of inventory, of which individually selling items of lesser value would take a lifetime. The higher value items are typically put in high end auctions and sold directly to antique dealers and collectors for premium prices. This is usually what is shown on the popular TV shows such as *Auction Hunters* and *Storage Wars*. On these TV shows you don't see what goes on behind the scenes, you only see the individual items pulled out and sold for huge profits. This is what sparks so many individuals to wanting to start buying storage auctions. It may be easy to flip the valuables but the novice buyer will struggle unloading the rest of the merchandise and may result to discarding it or reselling it for a fraction of the potential value.

Storage auction buyers will group their merchandise into lots and categories of items. Some of the items will be common household goods; other items may be small valuable collectibles, jewelry, office supplies, electronics, weapons, furniture, art and so forth. You have to learn how to move massive amounts of inventory in short periods of time. The household goods are best sold in box lots at consignment auctions. Many fairground auctions and consignment auctions will sell these types of goods. This will allow you to sell hundreds of items in a single sale and collect your payment and be done with it. Other slightly more valuable items may be sent to flea markets or put in large yard sales.

Posting an advertisement in the local classifieds section of a newspaper or penny saver for a swap meet or liquidation may be a good idea. You can find other resellers and dealers to exchange goods and services with as well as find potential buyers of merchandise. This may help you keep the storage space required to keep buying and flipping to a minimum.

eBay Trading Assistants and certified eBay Drop Off Outlets have also become a source of income for auction flippers. One can locate a mass community of consignors through eBay's portal. Personally I have owned an eBay Drop Off business and would be contacted by storage auction buyers, junk hauling companies and even real estate flippers because properties they purchased had massive amounts of inventory that needed to be flipped quickly. Finding yourself reliable and trustworthy trading assistants and eBay Drop Off Outlets will allow you a means of selling your reasonably valuable items in a fast paced environment. I have known storage auction buyers who used as many as five different eBay Trading Assistants to sell close to a thousand products a month. At the same time they were dropping off items to the local consignment auction, flea market, antique dealership and prestigious auction houses. They would then be able to sell certain high valuable collectibles and items to collectors that they had built relationships with over the years.

Using all of these different sales venues the auction flipper and offline reseller can many streams of passive income. Essentially they just need to drive around distributing merchandise to their sales channels. Once this process has been mastered it is possible to turn this into a business and on auto pilot. You can hire an individual to handle phone calls and contact dealers and venues about buying items directly and placing your merchandise in their stores or auctions. You can hire drivers to transport your goods from place to place. Lastly you will be able to just focus on buying merchandise at storage auctions, estate sales & auctions, business liquidations or other inventory sources.

Eventually if you're comfortable with someone else's ability to buy inventory at auction for you or your business than you will be able to step back and just collect money. Typically from what I have witnessed in the auction business is that auction flippers will have one main apprentice. This apprentice is commonly a son or daughter or other family member but it could be anyone trust worthy. They go to the auctions and study the process until they are eventually ready to take over. An example of this type of structure on TV is seen on the show Pawn Stars and is common in pawn store ownership with a father letting his sons or daughters work in the store getting a feel for the business. This allows the teacher to point out mistakes that will happen along the way and share experiences of past history in the business. When you are selling used goods most transactions will not be the same. It will be virtually impossible to know everything about ever item that comes into your shop or you purchase at auction. It will be more important to have a general knowledge about types of items of value, brand names of value and liquidity of items.

# Chapter 3 – Where & How to Buy

      Finding items to sell becomes easier and easier the longer you are in the game, eventually the items will start coming to even if you don't want them to. Through networking and word of mouth your family members will start asking you to sell things for them, your neighbors, friends and even other sellers you will run into. This can become annoying if you don't like dealing with people or you already have a massive inventory to sell. I constantly get phone calls from people asking me what something is worth or begging me to sell something for them. When I first started selling this was a great way for me to make money with no money down and can be extremely profitable if you are selling the right merchandise, especially if you are selling for a business. Lately I turn down these offers as I do great on my own but this is a great place to start if you don't have a lot of money but we will get into consignments shortly but first we will talk about making your first sales.

## Selling Personal Items

This is typically the best place to start; by selling your own items first you can get a better feel and understanding for the sales process and build confidence in your abilities. This way if you make some mistakes listing, or lose money shipping or get too little for your item you only have yourself to blame. Take a walk through your house or apartment and walk through each room, definitely check your closets, attic, shed and garage and gather up a few items that you don't use anymore and can do without. Make sure they are small enough and light enough to be shipped (don't try and sell a weight bench as your first item).

Some examples of simple items commonly found in the house that aren't used anymore would be a VCR, children's toys, tools, kitchen appliances, instruments, sports equipment, purses, shoes (you know you women have to many of them) etc. Here is where you will definitely want to have signed up for a research account, the one I recommend is Terapeak.com if you don't have an account with them or not ready to sign up with one you can try and look at prices and bids currently on eBay but the numbers may be deceiving as most items on eBay shoot up at the last minute or are sold in an eBay store which you won't be able to have access to those records. Assuming you have the Terapeak account, login and set the search to 90 days. Type in each item into the search; make sure you keep the search simple but accurate. For instance if you have a VCR you want to look up and potentially list don't do a search for "VCR" be specific, type the brand name and model number such as SONY STR-XXX VCR. If you have the remote with it, compare top results that include the remote, if you don't see what the prices are without one so you can get a better gauge of the true value of your item. Don't be discouraged if you see an item you have sell for a very low price and than others very high, there can be many factors for that such as a bad title, bad category, the item may be defective, bad time of the day or maybe it just did not attract the right buyers that week. After you are done researching your items and have found ones that you want to sell you can move onto the next Chapter if you're ready to start selling right now, if not go ahead and keep reading and comeback to them when you're finished.

# Consignments

This can be a great way to make money without spending any of your own; however this type of selling will require you to keep excellent records. Consignees, which are individuals or businesses that are agreeing to let you sell something for them without a money transaction upfront, fees are based on the successful sale of said items. This means that you will be the consignor in this agreement and you will in most cases take possession of the consignees items or inventory until the sale is completed at which time you will facilitate the sale to the customer. The consignor will handle all the money, deal with the customers directly and handle all aspects of the sales process. This means that the consignee is only responsible for providing the goods. As a consignor you are in a great position, you don't have to worry about a lot of overhead costs that would be associated with purchasing your own inventory with your own capital and hoping that it sells. You can eliminate a lot of the risks associated with retail as you won't need any starting capital to purchase inventory.

Consignees of goods can be found just about anywhere you look. Maybe your parents, grandparents or a relative has a garage full of tools or an attic full of collectibles and antiques that they would like to get rid of. Maybe your neighbor has a bunch of items that they would like to sell.

A prime source of usually untapped consignees is at yard sales, flea markets, hauling companies and storage auctions. Yard sales are very common and usually the individual(s) having the yard sale will have merchandise left over after the sale, they may also have other items they want to sell in the future. As a consignor you can drop off your business card, call them on the phone provided one is listed and explain your services to them and that you will help them sell any remaining items of value on a consignment basis. You can do the same exact thing at flea markets for vendors with excess goods. At storage auctions you can leave your card with buyers and dealers. Storage auction buyers will generally be very glad to have you helping them liquidate their stored up inventory. Be careful as these strategies may quickly create massive amounts of work for you to handle and you may be overloaded with inventory very quickly. Hauling companies are very easy to locate, you can check your local Yellow Pages or classifieds and find people and companies hauling all types of items. Typically hauling companies will also be willing to negotiate a deal for your consignment services as they will be hauling junk but also goods and merchandise from a variety of different sources. If they are smaller companies or even individuals they might not be aware of the potential resale value of these goods and you can fill in the blanks for them and let them know what types of inventory they should hold on to that you can sell for them.

eBay also offers a program known as eBay Trading Assistant and Registered eBay Drop Off Locations which can be an easy way for us to build up a client base of consignees. Anyone can become a trading assistant and this is a great place to start if you are new to selling or unsure about how involved you are ready to become in sales. Using the eBay Trading Assistant program local sellers and people will be able to search based on location for potential sellers and what types of items that you sell. You can setup your profile to only accept antique items, vintage items, automobiles and parts, electronics and so forth. You can setup your commission rate and offer completive percentages.

If you are interested in the eBay Registered Drop Off Location I will make your decision quick, do you have a physical store front? If not then you are not eligible as you will need a registered PHYSICAL business than you will not be eligible for this.

From person experience this program has been a great and valuable asset. When I ran a company that had many drop off locations we constantly received new customers and consignees as well as some major contracts with junk removal companies, second hand companies, real estate investors for estate liquidations, small business liquidations and people looking to sell personal and individual items.

To become an eBay Trading Assistant or a registered Drop Off Location sign up free here:
**http://ebaytradingassistant.com/directory/index.php?page=home**

Consignment contracts can be very easy to setup as many individuals and even businesses need to sell things from time to time. You need to be very confident in your abilities as salesman or woman. You should be able to prove to the

Example of Consignment Contract:

Dear (consignee name),

It's been extremely satisfying in dealing with you. On the basis of our progress moving forward it has been brought to light that we need to re-evaluate our consignment agreement.

As per our conversation on selling your merchandise under a consignment deal, we have come up with the following rates and services that we offer for all of our consignment contracts. The following is negotiable and can be discussed at a later date upon review. The terms are as follows:

Any item sold on eBay will be listed properly and with the guidance of the consignee to avoid any confusion on the base price, reserve price, and final price. Items sold under our company, under our eBay account must be chosen and approved by both parties before selling of said item commences.

While the buyer from eBay is held responsible for all shipping and handling fees, any profit that may be incurred from shipping is not split in our consignment agreement. The fees charged by eBay to our account for listing items will be held responsible by the consignee. These fees include listing, as well as final value fees. Our program will calculate all of these fees and a thorough breakdown for each item sold will be included on the end of month invoice calculation for items sold. If an item is not sold the first time we will list a second time, if the item does not sell a second time around, the consignee will decide whether the item should be grouped together with similar items for a third listing as a "lot". If the third listing is still unsuccessful, a final evaluation of whether to list the items again will be brought to the consignee. Once an item is listed for the first time, it will have a shelf life of no more than 35 days before it is either returned to the consignee or thrown into the trash. Receiving and Returning items will be handled under the consignees own abilities – we do not transport any items unless it is on route to a customer.

Upon a successful sale on eBay there will be a percentage split of the actual final price from eBay. These percentage splits are as follows:

Items sold for $1.00 - $500.00 will have a 50% split between the consignee and the consigner.
Items sold for $500.00 - $2000.00 will have a 60/40% split between the consignee and the consigner.
Items sold for $2000.00 - $5000.00 will have a 70/30% split between the consignee and the consigner. Items sold for $5000.00 and over will have a 80/20% split between the consignee and the consigner.

We can offer payment by Check will be mailed by the end of every month (30th or 31st) that includes the amount owed for our consignment agreement.

We will provide timely reports and will answer any questions you may have as we move forward. We offer a guarantee to try and get as much revenue as possible for your merchandise and while we are very good at determining fair and realistic prices for each item, we will not sell an item for any less than you think it should sell for. We can use a method of reserved pricing on eBay to make sure these reserves are met. As we progress further on this business endeavor we are looking forward to working with you.

Sincerely,

(Your name, title, company, contact info)

Here is another example of a contract that we used for one of my businesses:
Front of contract for drop off form:

**"The Easiest Way to Sell on eBay"**

## Drop-Off Form
(please fill in all fields)

First Name:_____ Last Name:_____

Street Address (no PO Boxes):_____

City:_____ State:_____ Zip Code:_____ Ph. No.:_____

Email:_____

**Item Information:**
1) Manufacturer/Brand Name:_____ Model Name/Number:_____

Description (features, accessories, age, size, color, etc.):_____
_____

Estimated Value: $_____ Listing Selection: ☐ Basic    ☐ Premium **(Starting Price: $_____)**

2) Manufacturer/Brand Name:_____ Model Name/Number:_____

Description (features, accessories, age, size, color, etc.):_____
_____

Estimated Value: $_____ Listing Selection: ☐ Basic    ☐ Premium **(Starting Price: $_____)**

3) Manufacturer/Brand Name:_____ Model Name/Number:_____

Description (features, accessories, age, size, color, etc.):_____
_____

Estimated Value: $_____ Listing Selection: ☐ Basic    ☐ Premium **(Starting Price: $_____)**

**Listing Options:**

|  | Basic | Premium |
|---|---|---|
| Auction Duration | 7 Day | 3, 5, 7, or 10 days |
| Photos | 1 Gallery Photo | 3 Photos |
| Starting Price | $1.00 | Your Choice |
| Sales Fee* | 30% of the first $300 + 18% of the remaining amount | 34% of the first $300 + 20% of the remaining amount |
| Listing Fee | $5.00 per Item Listed | $5.00 per Item Listed |

*Listing fee will be deducted from Sales Fee upon completion of the auction. Minimum Sales Fee shall be $5.00.

**Date and signature:**
Your signature below constitutes your agreement to be bound by the terms and conditions listed on both sides of this agreement. You authorize Bay4Pay and its partners to send you emails related to this transaction.

Signature:_____

Today's Date: _____

## Terms and Conditions

1.  **Services.** By signing this agreement you (the "Seller") authorize (NetDirectSales, Inc ("Bay4Pay") to provide the following services (the "Services") in accordance with the terms and conditions of this agreement: to (a) receive and store the goods listed on the reverse page (the "Goods"); (b) list and offer the Goods for sale on eBay; (c) deliver the Goods to the prevailing buyer, if any; and (d) collect the sales price from the buyer, deduct Bay4Pay sales fee and forward the remainder of the sales price to Seller in accordance with the terms and conditions set forth below.

2.  **Rights.** By signing this agreement, Seller confirms that he or she is at least 18 years of age, is the sole legal owner of the Goods, and has the right to sell the Goods.

3.  **Binding Bids.** Seller is obligated to complete the transaction with the highest bidder upon the listing's completion unless there is an exceptional circumstance such as (a) the buyer fails to pay for the Goods, or (b) Bay4Pay cannot authenticate the buyer's identity.

4.  **Unsold Goods.** Should the Goods fail to sell after being listed on eBay, Seller hereby agrees to collect the unsold Goods ("Unsold Goods") at the Drop-off location no later than 7 days after delivery of notification by Bay4Pay that the Unsold Goods are available for pick up. If the Unsold Goods are not collected within 7 days from notification, Seller hereby authorizes Bay4Pay to dispose of Unsold Goods without providing compensation therefor to Seller.

5.  **Payment to Seller.** As consideration for the Services, Seller agrees Bay4Pay will be entitled to deduct from the purchase price of the Goods a sales fee ("Sales Fee") according to the following formula: for Basic Service (as selected by the Seller), the Sales Fee shall be thirty percent (30%) of the price for which the Goods are sold (the "Sales Price") up to a Sales Price of $300.00 plus eighteen percent (18%) of the remaining Sales Price over $300.00 or $5.00, whichever amount is greater, plus all eBay listing and final value fees plus all PayPal payment processing fees. For Premium Service (as selected by the Seller), the Sales Fee shall be thirty four percent (34%) of the price Sales Price up to a Sales Price of $300.00 plus twenty percent (20%) of the remaining Sales Price over $300.00 or $5.00, whichever amount is greater, plus all eBay listing and final value fees plus all PayPal payment processing fees. Following receipt by Bay4Pay of the Sales Price from the buyer, Bay4Pay is authorized by Seller to deduct the Sales Fee from the monies received and forward the remainder to Seller at the address listed on the reverse page, within fourteen (14) days from date of item shipment.

6.  **Bailment Relationship.** The relationship between Bay4Pay and the Seller is that of bailor and bailee in which the bailee (Seller) deposits his personal property (Goods) with the bailor (Bay4Pay) for the purpose of listing and selling the Goods to third parties through eBay. Nothing contained herein will be construed as creating an agency, partnership, or other form of joint enterprise between the parties.

7.  **Title and Risk of Loss.** After being packaged by the Seller, item is insured for the value designated by Seller up to $5,000, the cost of which will be paid by Bay4Pay on behalf of Seller from the Sales Price. Title will not transfer to Bay4Pay at any time. Title to shipped Goods will pass directly from Seller to Buyer.

8.  **Seller's Warranty of Goods.** Seller warrants that (a) Seller has all the necessary rights and authorization to produce and distribute the Goods to any third party; (b) the Goods and the rights granted under this agreement do not infringe the proprietary rights of any third party; (c) the description of the Goods is truthful, accurate, and complete and not be false, inaccurate, or misleading; (d) there has been no fraudulent activity with respect to the Goods and neither the Goods nor the attempted or actual sale thereof involves the sale or transfer of counterfeit or stolen items; (e) the sale or transfer of the Goods by Seller on eBay does not violate any law, statute, ordinance, or regulation (including, but not limited to, those governing export control, consumer protection, unfair competition, antidiscrimination or false advertising; (f) nothing in the description of the Goods or in the Goods themselves is defamatory, trade libelous, unlawfully threatening, unlawfully harassing or obscene; and (g) neither the description nor the Goods contains child pornography or other content that is adult in nature or harmful to minors.

9.  **Breach.** Without limiting other remedies, Bay4Pay may immediately remove the Goods' listings from eBay, temporarily suspend or terminate the Services and refuse to provide future services to Seller if: (a) Seller breaches this agreement, (b) Bay4Pay is unable to verify or authenticate any information Seller provides to Bay4Pay, (c) Bay4Pay believes that Seller's actions may cause financial loss or legal liability for Seller, Bay4Pays' users or Bay4Pay, or (d) Bay4Pay suspects that Seller (by conviction, settlement, insurance or escrow investigation, or otherwise) has engaged in fraudulent activity in connection with the Goods, Bay4Pay, eBay, or otherwise.

10. **Indemnity.** Seller agrees to indemnify, defend and hold Bay4Pay and its parent, subsidiaries, affiliates, officers, directors, agents, members and employees, harmless from any loss, claim or demand, including reasonable attorneys' fees, connected to or arising out of Seller's breach of this agreement, or Seller's violation of any law or the rights of any third party.

11. **Warranty Disclaimer.** Bay4Pay provides its services "as is" and without any warranty or representation as to the Services, express, implied or statutory. Bay4Pay specifically disclaims any implied warranties of title, merchantability, fitness for a particular purpose and non-infringement. Some states do not allow the disclaimer of implied warranties, so the foregoing disclaimer may not apply to Seller. This warranty gives Seller specific legal rights and Seller may also have other legal rights that vary from State to State.

12. **Waiver of Consequential Damages.** IN NO EVENT WILL BAY4PAY BE LIABLE TO SELLER FOR ANY INCIDENTAL , CONSEQUENTIAL, EXEMPLARY, INDIRECT, SPECIAL, OR PUNITIVE DAMAGES ARISING OUT OF THIS AGREEMENT OR ITS TERMINATION, REGARDLESS OF THE FORM OF ACTION (INCLUDING NEGLIGENCE AND STRICT PRODUCT LIABILITY) AND IRRESPECTIVE OF WHETHER BAY4PAY HAS BEEN ADVISED OF THE POSSIBILITY OF ANY SUCH LOSS OR DAMAGE.

13. **Liability Cap.** Bay4Pay's liability, and the liability of its employees and suppliers, to Seller or any third parties in any circumstance is limited to $100. Some states do not allow the exclusion or limitation of incidental or consequential damages, so the above limitation or exclusion may not apply to Seller.

14. **Release.** Seller releases Bay4Pay, eBay and their respective officers, directors, agents, subsidiaries, joint ventures and employees) from claims, demands, and damages (actual and consequential) of every kind and nature, known and unknown, suspected and unsuspected, disclosed and undisclosed, arising out of, resulting from or in any way connected with the Services. If Seller is a California resident, Seller waives California Civil Code § 1542, which says: "A general release does not extend to claims which the creditor does not know or suspect to exist in his favor at the time of executing the release, which if known by him must have materially affected his settlement with the debtor."

15. **Term.** The term of this agreement will commence upon the date hereof and unless terminated earlier in accordance with the terms of this agreement, will continue until all Goods accepted for listing by Bay4Pay under this agreement are sold and delivered, returned to Seller, or disposed of in accordance with Section 3, but in no event more than sixty (60) days from the date hereof. This agreement may be terminated by Bay4Pay without notice, for any reason or no reason, at any time. If Bay4Pay terminates this agreement and returns the Goods or the Sale Price net of the Sales Fee to Seller, Seller shall have no further recourse against Bay4Pay .

16. **Survival of Certain Terms.** The following Sections will survive the termination of this agreement for any reason: 3,5,6,7,8,9,10,11,12,13, 14, 15 and 16. All other rights and obligations of the parties will cease upon termination of this agreement.

17. **General.** This agreement will be governed in all respects by the laws of the United States of America and the State of Maryland as such laws are applied to agreements entered into and to be performed entirely with Maryland between Maryland residents. All notices or requests will be in writing and will be sent by facsimile, or recognized commercial overnight courier, at which time they will be deemed to have been delivered. Notices will be deemed received upon receipt of written confirmation of transmission when sent by facsimile, or signing for receipt of delivery if sent by overnight courier. Notices will be sent to the parties at the address set forth in the signature block, below. The failure of either party to require performance by the other party of any provision hereof will not affect the full right to require such performance at any time thereafter; nor will the waiver by either party of a breach of any provision hereof be taken or held to be a waiver of the provision itself. In the event that any provision of this agreement will be unenforceable or invalid under any applicable law, or be so held by applicable court decision, such unenforceability or invalidity will not render this agreement unenforceable or invalid as a whole, and, in such event, such provisions will be changed and interpreted so as to best accomplish the objectives of such unenforceable or invalid provision within the limits of applicable law or applicable court decisions. This agreement and any exhibits hereto, constitute the entire agreement between the parties with respect to the subject matter hereof. This agreement supersedes, and the terms of this agreement govern, any prior or collateral agreements with respect to the subject matter hereof with the exception of any prior confidentiality agreements between the [  ] mutual agreement of authorized representatives of the parties in writing.

# Yard Sales

Yard sales and garage sales are such a great resource for the beginning reseller to the expert reseller. They provide a means to meet potential clients and create business partnerships, as well as providing negotiable prices. My roots in sales started from yard sales and still to this day if I see one as I am driving I write down locations and times that are usually posted on stop signs and telephone poles of future sales.

Typically you will see most yard sales held in the spring and summer but you can find them year round depending where you live and what the weather is like. Most of the time yard sales will be held on Saturday and Sunday's early in the morning from about 9:00 AM to 1:00 or 2:00 PM. Yard sales will typically give us a great ROI which is our return on investment. You will be able to pick up many items for five to ten bucks that are worth at least fifty to a hundred. If you start buying a lot of items from one location a seller may also offer you other items that they have in their house that you may be interested in. You will also have a chance to leave a business card or at least leave you phone number with the seller and let them know if they still have items left after the sale or they want to unload items in the future to give you a call. This goes back to what we discussed previously based on consignment sales and this certainly is a great way to locate future consignees. Typically when we are purchasing electronics and other items that we may not be able to test we can ask the seller directly if it is fully functional, most likely they will not lie about the condition of an item if you know where they live, sometimes if they are not too busy or if the item is of great value they will be more than willing to test it out for you and show you it is a great item. Besides driving around looking for signs posted about sales there are some great sites online and local print magazines and papers you should check. A great one that comes in print and online is the Pennysaver, they have an online site at Pennysaverwired.com. You can search your local area for yard sale listings to find dates, times and the types of items that may be sold at the location.

Another great place to check out is www.craigslist.org which is a great free classified listing site. You will also be able to find listings in your area and sometimes contact sellers before hand to ask them questions about sales. Craigslist can be a great way to get a preview of the merchandise before anyone else or even make them an offer to buy the contents outright before the sale even goes down. You can also check your local paper for listings and there are some other good online sites that offer searchable databases for local yard sales. Even if you miss a yard sale or you arrive to late, it does not hurt to knock on the door of the seller and ask them if they have anything left to sell, you may be surprised at how cheap they will sell you remaining items.

There are typically four types of yard sales that I look for; the first is a "moving sale". At a moving sale you should have the best thing in the world for a buyer and that is a motivated seller! If this is a true moving sale that means that the seller typically has to get rid of certain items that they do not want to take with them in the move. This should create extremely low prices and negotiating prices should be a breeze. If you go to one of these sales first thing in the morning and they are not willing to negotiate, come back toward the end of their sale and usually they will change their tune and be much more susceptive to selling at a lower price, this philosophy should also hold true for just about all types of yard sales. It does not hurt to double back and see if a seller has put out more items or is willing to negotiate for what they have left. A lot of the time if you check yard sale and moving sale listings toward the end of college semesters you will find college students that are trying to get rid of their items out of their dorm rooms. Many times at college campuses you will see loads of students' simply trashing items they don't want to take back home or they are studying abroad and can't take them home – however this creates a feeding frenzy amongst dumpster divers!

The second type I look for would be multi-family yard sales or community yard sales, definitely take note of these. At this type of sale usually many families in a neighborhood or apartment complex will bring out items they want to sell. This gives us a lot of flexibility when looking for good deals, if a seller at one location is not willing to negotiate or their prices are already way to high then you can move on to the next table or house in the area.

Rummage sales are the next type of sale I definitely make note of and will sometimes a fair distance for if they are not in my area. These are typically held at churches and Schools and these usually consist of church members donating their items for a good cause and a tax write off. The ones typically held at schools are done by the PTA members or sports teams in order for the team or school to do some fundraising. Typically the ones held at the churches are handled by the church members and their staff and negotiations are limited sometimes but the prices are usually amazing because the sellers have no attachment to the items and are simply just trying to raise money. School sales will sometimes be a little higher priced and you may have to deal with individual sellers at perspective tables. However the quality of inventory found at the school and church sales is typically lower level so don't expect to spend or make a ton of money at these. Typically I will end up buying five to ten items at an individual sale and spending less than a hundred dollars.

My favorite and fourth type of sale that you should be on the lookout for is estate/yard sales. In this scenario typically you see family members trying to hold their own estate sale of someone who passed away or is elderly. They basically are looking to sell the contents of the house and you can make offers on just about anything inside. These are rather rare to find, often you will see this sales listed and you show up and they have been falsely advertised and represented and will just be people holding yard sales and not selling off their entire estate. However, if you find one that truly is an estate sale you may just find yourself a gold mine. I have found Rolexes, Gold jewelry, Cars & Parts, Tools and some great antiques that were being offered for pennies on the dollar. In some cases you can fill up bags and boxes with as much as you can fit from someone's attic, basement or garage because they simply want it gone. I must repeat though that these types of sales are often rare and they can sometimes draw a nice crowd but you should have a much better buying opportunity from a personally held estate sale than many of the ones you will find done by professionals. The professionals know what items are worth and they work on commission so you better know what you're doing, I will get into true estate sales later.

# Thrift Stores

Thrift stores and second hand stores present a unique buying opportunity for us resellers. I have visited over a hundred different thrift stores in my time across ten different states, primarily on the east coast of the United States. At virtually every stop that I have been to there has been buying opportunities to be found, regardless if I made a purchase or not. Most thrift stores will have special savings days or some form of discount pricing. For instance there is a thrift store that I frequent when I am in the area, typically once a month or so and they mark their inventory with a lettering system A,B,C,D,E and it is done by the week that the item was received in. An item would be marked with an A and a price, four weeks later the thrift store would change their rotating sign to "Items marked with A are 50% off". I have seen many stores with a very similar system, some other ones with have things like 25% clothes on Saturdays, 25% off electronics on Wednesday, buy one get one Sunday on collectibles, etc. The trick with thrift stores is to find those killer deep discount deals for maximum profits. If the thrift store is local and you have time to visit it frequently than you can figure out their pricing strategies and make note of items that you may be interested in purchasing if the price is reduced.

Here are a few examples of some items that can be found in most thrift stores, at least ones around my neck of the woods. This was a basic sheet of what I would commonly purchase when I was flat broke trying to take back my life. I had to use a credit card with a very low limit at this time in my life but I could drive around all day visiting all the thrift stores in my area and make a $1000 from spending $200 or less.

| Item Description | Brand Names | Price | Resale |
|---|---|---|---|
| Treasure Chest Jewelry Boxes | | $10 | $20-$75 |
| NFL,NBA,NHL,MLB JERSEYS | Adidas, NIKE, Reebok, Champion | $10 | $20-$80 |
| Hunting Clothes | Cabelas | $5 | $20-$50 |
| HI-FI VCRS | Sony, Emerson | $10 | $25-$75 |
| Betamax VCR | Sony | $30 | $50-$300 |
| VCR - NEW IN BOX | Any Known Name Brand | $40 | $100+ |
| Laser Printers | HP, Samsung, Brother, Xerox | $35 | $50-$300 |
| Photo Printers | Canon, HP, EPSON | $10 | $40-$200 |
| Bread Makers | Zojirushi | $30 | $50-$200 |
| Pasta Makers | Lello, Atlas, KitchenAid | $20 | $75-$200 |
| Crepe/Pizelle Makers | | $5 | $25-$50 |
| Silverware SILVERPLATE Sets | Reed & Barton, F.B. Rogers | $25 | $50-$200 |
| Food Vacuum Sealers | FoodSaver | $10 | $20-$200 |
| China Sets | Wedgwood, Lenox, Royal Worcester | | |
| Vacuum Cleaners | Rainbow, Bosch, Kirby, Gaia, Dyson, Oreck | | $50-$200+ |
| Power Tools | DeWalt, Snap-on, Makita,Ridgid,Bosch,Stanley | | |
| Super Soaker Water Guns | Super Soaker Models 50, 100 | $10 | $40-$150 |
| Toy Trucks | HESS, Tonka, Nylint, Dinky Toys, Lincol | $5 | |
| Model Cars | Revell, ERTL, Danbury Mint | $5 | |

Here is what my average thrift store purchase looks like, this cost me $103, the VCR's were $3 each and I resold the entire purchase from an hour's work for over $1100!

Here is a shot of just a few of the VCR's that I flipped on Amazon (Date Closed is sold date) the rest was sold throughout various other marketplaces. Just to show you what kind of profit you can turn with a few dollars:

| | Actions | Merchant SKU | ASIN/ISBN | Product Name | Date Closed | Quantity | Condition | Your Price | Low Price | Status | Fulfilled By |
|---|---|---|---|---|---|---|---|---|---|---|---|
| | | ▽ | | ▽ | ▽ | ▽ | | ▽ | | | |
| | Actions ▼ | BX-40U9-DJ3Y | B00005V9Q3 | Panasonic PV-V4922 4-Head Mono VCR [Electronics] | 09/23/2011 04:01:45 | 0 | Used - Very Good | $74.99 | | Closed (Out of Stock) | Merchant |
| | Actions ▼ | XH-YADU-NZ7X | B00000IXV4 | Panasonic PV-9451 Hi-Fi VCR with VCR Plus+ [Electronics] | 09/21/2011 14:16:36 | 0 | Used - Very Good | $109.99 | | Closed (Out of Stock) | Merchant |
| | Actions ▼ | XH-IOU7-NUMH | B00008VEK8 | JVC HRJ692U 4-Head Hi-Fi VCR , Black [Electronics] | 08/17/2011 19:18:41 | 0 | Used - Very Good | $59.99 | | Closed (Out of Stock) | Merchant |
| | Actions ▼ | JB-QFCC-85R8 | B000O5O7LK | RCA VR623 4-Head HiFi Stereo VCR [Electronics] | 07/22/2011 23:00:47 | 0 | Used - Good | $49.99 | | Closed (Out of Stock) | Merchant |
| | Actions ▼ | HJ-4F8L-F4WD | B00006CFLU | Memorex MVR4052 4-Head Hi-Fi VCR [Electronics] | 07/14/2011 17:49:15 | 0 | Used - Very Good | $49.99 | | Closed (Out of Stock) | Merchant |
| | Actions ▼ | 5I-FHOX-YSMW | B00005A0QW | Panasonic PV-V4611 4-Head Hi-Fi Stereo VCR [Electronics] | 07/03/2011 21:20:37 | 0 | Used - Very Good | $88.99 | | Closed (Out of Stock) | Merchant |
| | Actions ▼ | 2H-OC3Q-2WLO | B00005V9Q4 | Panasonic PV-V4522 4-Head Hi-Fi VCR [Electronics] | 07/03/2011 11:43:55 | 0 | Used - Good | $88.99 | $85.00 | Closed (Out of Stock) | Merchant |

On the VCRs alone that is gross sales of $523 and with shipping charge total gross $615. The cost of the VCRs was $26, so my initial gross profit before subtracting fees and shipping cost is $589.

# Estate Sales

Estate sales are liquidation sales of an individual's property after they have passed away in most cases but can also be held if someone is moving or in rare cases to liquidate some quick assets to pay off debts. Typically when a person passes away family members will hire a company to handle the liquidation of the estate in order to divide up the funds. Estate sales generally include everything located on the property of the individual, including the house, vehicles and possessions. Estate sales differ from yard sales and garage sales because they are run by a company or a third party to handle the sale and will include the sale of everything. It may also be harder to bargain at an estate sale depending on the company running it. Generally you will see estate sale run for three days, usually starting on Friday and ending Sunday. The first day of the sale there are no discounts most of the time, the second day you will typically see 25% off of everything and the final day is usually 50% off with the ability for deep deals and negotiations. Items that are not sold during the estate sale liquidation period are generally consigned to an estate auction company. The estate auction company will also buy the items outright in many cases and resell them at their local auction house.

In order to locate true estate sales it can be a good idea to do some searches in your local area for estate sale companies and sign up for their newsletter and mailing list if they offer one. Another easy method is to search sites such as EstateSales.net and Estatesales.org as well as Craigslist.org. Be sure to check who is holding the sale, you will commonly see people having yard sales and listing them as estate sales when in reality they are only selling a few items. I suggest checking out many different estate sales held by different companies in order to get a better feel of how well they are organized, how they price items and if they negotiate or not. Generally we want to find estate sales that are held by inexperienced people and companies that are not well organized. Companies that have a lot of employees on hand and laptops setup all over the place generally price items very high and do a lot of market research on the items that they are selling. This makes buying and reselling a lot more difficult as we may only find a few items that are reasonably priced.

The typical strategy that I use for estate sales is I get there bright and early the first day they hold the sale. I bring a pen and notepad to write on and I write down prices and descriptions of items that I am not familiar with and will either go back to my car or to my house to do research on the items before making a purchase. If I have access to the entire house I love to look in closets, drawers, cabinets and other enclosed places to try and find items that the estate company has not gone through yet. On many occasions I have found valuables that were hidden away and presented them to the associate in charge at the sale and asked for a combined price on these items and received incredible deals on the spot as they will not have time to research properly. Keep in mind that many estate sale companies will use ropes, tape and other means to close off certain areas of the house and property and you will not be able to buy items located there. During the first day of the sale I generally do not make a lot of purchases unless the prices are already great or the company is willing to negotiate and combine items for deals.

Rarely will I come back to the same sale the second day unless I had done research later the first day and found item(s) that would be worth my time going back for and were at a great risk of being picked up by another buyer. It has been my experience that the first day of the sale, especially if it is held on a Friday will have far less people walking through to buy so many items you may have been interested in will still be available the second day. You can always call the estate company and ask them if an item has been sold or not. The second day of the sale, if it is held on a Saturday will usually draw a very large crowd so if you did not make it the first day you should plan on being at the sale as soon as it opens the next day.

The last day of the sale is usually the most profitable for us resellers, the estate company will be looking to unload everything they can and prices are almost always cut in half. If you are purchasing multiple items you should ask for another discount, I have purchased entire rooms full of items for half price on already half prices. If you are a social individual try and strike up some conversations with other buyers at the estate sales, find out what companies estate sales they like the best, what the prices are like and negotiating information.

In 2006 after I had just lost everything I owned and was bankrupted, I had $100 left in my pocket and I found an estate sale that was unorganized and was letting customers fill up banker boxes to the top for $10, whatever you could find in the basement and garages. I filled up three boxes with a carburetor for a Studebaker car, distributors for a rare corvette, trimmers and shears for sheep, a ribbon maker and car manuals. I spent $30 and sold the contents of the items for over $2000! If you are patient and aggressive, buying a lot of items on the cheap you can be extremely profitable.

# Onsite Liquidation Auctions

Onsite auctions typically happen when a company goes out of business or is shutting down, but they also happen in order for the company to clear out old or used inventory. They also happen when someone dies and an auction company will auction off the contents of the house, known as chattels to the highest bidder. When the contents are sold it is typically done so as one lot and this is where many of your local auction companies get their inventory from and then they resell everything individually at their auction house. I have not personally won any onsite estate liquidation sales, but I have been to several just to see what the prices were like. This book will not cover the purchase of these types of sales because they require massive storage capabilities and fast resale, as well as rather high prices. The range of prices from the few estate liquidations that I have been too were from around $1500 to $28,000 and I am sure they go much higher if rare art and antiques are there.

Business liquidation auctions happen to be one of my favorite auctions to attend. I do recommend bringing a large sum of cash if it is a cash only auction as many of them will be. You will want to check the terms of the auction with the auction company holding the sale, not the business whose inventory is being sold off. Some examples of onsite liquidation auctions that I have attended are thrift stores, pawn shops, car dealers, antique stores and electronic outlets. The auctioneers generally move extremely quickly and I have seen as many as fifteen hundred items sold off in a single day. There are a few disadvantages that we will face at most of these types of sales. Usually we will not have a chance to do proper research on the items we will be bidding on so the more general pricing information you know or have at your disposal the better you will do at these sales. You will be surprised sometimes when an item you think is relatively worthless ends up selling for a thousand dollars and most people at the auction will laugh that someone overpaid. However this is usually not the case, many dealers and resellers will be at these auctions and chances are they know exactly what the item is worth. I was recently at a cash only pawn store auction and I had brought $5,000 and already spent about $4,000 half way through the auction. Sure enough the auctioneer goes into the back and pulls out a 1930's Martin D-28 acoustic guitar and my heart started racing out of my chest knowing the potential value of these guitars. If you do a quick search using Terapeak.com or Google you will see that in nice condition some can fetch over $50,000 and this one was almost flawless. My jaw dropped after the horrible description that was given by the auctioneer for the guitar "Old Martin Acoustic Guitar". Having been to so many auctions in the past and knowing virtually all of the big time players and dealers in my area I quickly surveyed the room and the competition. I did not see anyone I was worried about until I looked in the corner and an old friend of mine and dealer who I routinely bid against for guitars and instruments waved at me. The bidding began and stalled at $300 with myself having the high bid and my heart feeling like it was going to beat through my chest now, then I hear "$500" from the corner and I realize that my dealer friend knows exactly what is up for sale. I counter with $700 and he takes it to $1000, now I know I cannot literally afford at that moment to pay for the item, especially with the buyers premium included in my buying thus far but I also know there are a few more guitars left to be sold and that this dealer is not likely to back down anytime soon. So I yell out, $1500 as to try and act as if I won't be bullied, he makes it $2000 and one final time I hit him again and make it $2500 and instantly he makes it $3000. The auctioneer paused for a few minutes and tried to entice me to continue bidding but I had to back down, the buyers at the auction all applauded our bidding war and had about twenty questions from people interested in what just happened and why we were bidding so high. However in the short term my mission was accomplished, while I was extremely disappointed that I did not win the guitar which is worth many people's yearly salary, I was able to take a nice hit to this dealer's bankroll that he had brought to the auction (he is worth several million so there was no long term damage). Upon winning the guitar the dealer immediately paid his bill and yelled over at me "the rest is yours…" which made me somewhat happy and I ended up purchasing eight more guitars for my remaining thousand dollars which I would resell for about $4000. In total I spent $5000 at the pawn store, I resold it for $15,560 and after fees from selling and a few refunds I was still able to net around $8000 profit for a weeks' worth of work listing and shipping.

I would run into the dealer again who purchased the Martin guitar and he showed me a receipt he had in his car from a local guitar collector's auction he had resold the Martin at, I looked down and had to do a double take as it read $37,600. I then immediately asked him what he was going to bid up to at the auction for the guitar, and he replied that he only had $4000 in his pocket and I thought I was going to vomit. My initial plan was to bring $10000 cash to the auction but it was not in the best part of town and carrying that kind of cash in a bad section of town without a concealed weapons permit makes me extremely nervous. Sometimes without taking great risks we won't receive great rewards. The other thing I learned, and have had to learn on many occasions at cash only auctions is that sometimes it is better to conserve your money until later in the auction in case something great comes up for sale. Also by being conservative with your money early in any auction may award you the time to feel out your competition and let them spend most of their money early on as many people are anxious and will routinely overbid in the beginning. They may also be overbidding early to send a message to the rest of the buyers at the auction that they have money and you won't win when they are bidding.

However by avoiding bidding wars and bidding with our mind, not our hearts and being patient we may just get an opportunity later when the crowd has thinned and people have over spent to win items very cheap. Most of the time I avoid bidding in the beginning of an auction unless I am trying to let people know that I can't be bullied around or there is just something really great that I can make money on in the beginning.

## Estate Auctions

### Auction Terms to be Understood:

## Absentee Bidding/Left Bids

If you are unable to attend an auction, you may leave an absentee bid. This is a confidential, **maximum** price for the lot or lots in which you are interested. It is executed by the auctioneer, on your behalf, in competition with the auction audience. In the event that your absentee bid is the winning bid for an item, you will be notified within a day of the auction.

## Buyer's Premium

The buyer's premium is a charge paid by the buyer at auction, usually in the form of a percentage of the winning bid or sold price of the lot. The buyer's premium may vary from auction to auction, and may include a discount for cash payment. The premium is paid at the time of purchase of the items bought at auction. For the specific amount, please view the details for each auction or ask the auctioneer.

Estate auctions saved my life, after losing everything I owned in 2006 I had $100 cash left. I went to a local estate auction and was able to purchase a box of items for $2 that had a set of vintage Aurora slot cars in it; I than purchased a cast iron antique train set for $5 and my final purchase was a Fenton cast iron wagon. I sold the Aurora cars for $655, the cast iron train set for $245 and the Fenton toy wagon for $570.

Estate Auctions are my favorite type of inventory acquisition mechanism as of late. You can find daily list of auction times, locations, terms and usually pictures of upcoming items by zip code on AuctionZip.com. You will see a calendar for auctions in your area; you can modify the search to extend your potential region. When I talk about estate auctions I am specifically talking about table lot style and warehouse floor auctions. I do not mean sit down paddle style auctions with a bunch of rich snobs which you will certainly find at auction houses like Christies and Sotheby's and such in New York.

At a table lot estate auction and sometimes consignment auctions, a group of bidders gathers around a table full of items or a line of items presented on the floor of a warehouse or auction house. In these types of auctions there are no reserve prices, a bidder can typically choose to hold up several items to bid on for one price if nobody objects. This allows for deep discounted price buying. When all of the bidding comes to a half at a specific table or row of items generally at most auction houses the auctioneer will sell the remainder of the lot or row of items. This is where small budget bidders can purchase a quantity of items for sometimes as low as a dollar. There will sometimes be seasoned resellers and owners of thrift stores and second hand stores that will almost always bid on these.

If you pay attention closely to the first few lots that are sold off you may spot one of these buyers, typically they will not take lightly to new bidders coming in and bidding against them on these lots and may make it costly for you to win one. However, buyers of these cheap left over lots usually will not have deep pockets and will fold if you keep bidding against them but don't be surprised if they make some smart remarks or try and get in your head after a bid. These buyers usually have typically been in the business for some time and many will consider these types of lots to be their territory.

If you are going to frequent the same estate auctions it is a good idea to get to know the regulars, being polite with them and making note of the types of items they purchase is a good idea. If you are constantly bidding against the same people when you purchase a certain type of item, then making friends with them might increase your profits and save you a lot of money. For instance there are several auctions in my area that I go to regularly and there is a group of buyers that I know very well and each of them I met through costly bidding wars with them. Many years ago when I was still new to auction houses the regular bidders saw me as a "newbie" and would team up against me to run up the prices of items I would bid on hoping to take away my will to bid against them. I was bidding against a tough crowd, I caught a few of them trying to "hit me" in retaliation to my bids against them. For example what I mean by this, one time I picked up a clock and opened the bid at $5 and one of the regulars immediately bid again to $10 and I backed out and he laughed at me and handed me the clock. He then told me that he was just trying to run the price up on me and he didn't have any interest in the item. He also taught me the ropes and strategies of becoming a successful auction buyer. Up until this point in my life I had really only been an experienced storage unit auction buyer, and when I was bidding on storage units I was doing it for my company and therefore I would have a fixed limit I would bid on certain types of units and I was not concerned with what other buyers did or how they acted. There were regulars at the storage auctions don't get me wrong, but at each auction there is typically only a handful of units to bid on and being friendly to other bidders is not as big of a concern as with other auctions.

Estate auctions will generally have hundreds to thousands of items to bid on in a single auction. If you bid on a hundred different items at a single auction to your maximum bid, even if you only win a few of them you will certainly attract a lot of unwanted attention. If there are not an abundance of new bidders at the auctions I frequent I can generally buy many items for close to nothing because of the relationships and understandings I have learned to develop with other buyers. For instance, before an auction starts I will typically hang around some of the big time buyers and dealers and we will talk about what we are interested in bidding on, defects of items, whether or not something is a reproduction or even potential resale values of items. Regulars will frequently meet and discuss amongst themselves and with other regulars what they are interested in bidding on and to get a feel for what the other regulars are interested in, the word usually gets spread around and a silent code is usually implied. The code is to share the bidding and not be too greedy.  If there are five clocks on the table that I would love to have and there is an abundance of other items that I am interested in bidding on later in the auction I will try and let my friends or regulars have a few and not bid against them, in return they will do the same for me. In this scenario the regulars are like a pack of piranhas feeding, one piranha does not eat everything but instead they take turns bidding. Piranhas usually stick together and will certainly attack any other fish in the sea and from time to time take bites out of each other but not eat each other unless there is not enough food to go around. The same philosophy is generally applied to the auction, regulars will occasionally bid against each other but they won't get into continuous battles against each other. Since I am now a reseller as a hobby and not for survival I don't need to be greedy and try and take everything and it is far more profitable to work together. However when there is very little bid on and everyone is interested in the same things than it can be everyone for themselves. These are not fixed rules you have to follow, just one potential strategy.

There is another auction that I frequent regularly that hundreds of people show up for and there are several thousand items that are sold off and I assume the shark or lone wolf strategy. There are many people that I know and am friendly with at this auction but I know that my pockets are far deeper than the majority of theirs and therefore I make no alliances or packs. At this auction the quality of the general merchandise is typically a bit lower than others I attend and if I want an item I will generally bid up to as high as I feel I can safely make a good profit and there are so many people in the room bidding that generally I cannot even see who I am bidding against.

The lone wolf or shark strategy is one that I use for estate and consignment auctions that implement a *bid for choice* auction format. In this format items are presented in table lots or rows as discussed previously but instead of a bidder picking up an item for the group to bid on, the bidder bids to their highest amount for choice of any item in the particular row or table. This style of auction is generally implemented when there are a great number of items that need to be auctioned off in a short period of time. I have also seen this strategy implemented with very small auctions and this is typically done to try and squeeze out the most money from these items as possible. Strategy, knowledge and research definitely come more into play in this auction format than with individual item bidding. Auctioneers use bid for choice to try and get buyers to all bid up to their maximum amount for a particular lot or row in hopes that the buyers are after different items. Many buyers will panic if there is an item in the row they want and believe someone else may grab the item if they allow them to get the bid for choice while the item is still available. This is when experience comes into play and knowledge of your competition as well as general product values is a key factor. If you know what the most valuable item in the row or lot is and it is not the item you are interested in, you can avoid bidding in the first round and see what the max bid in the crowd is. This can save you a lot of money by allowing higher bids to take the more valuable items and may give you a chance to wait and grab your item(s) at a more reasonable price.

The high bidder in bid for choice auctions will have the option of taking as many items as they like at that price, generally after that the auctioneer will offer the crowd the option to purchase as many items as they would like at the same price. Bidders will then have to be the first one to hold their bidder number up before other bidders to be next in line to make a pick. When the price for choice gets low enough, you cannot hesitate as there may be many interested parties waiting to snatch up bargains.

Auction houses may switch between bid for choice and

bid for a specific item, especially if they have a table of similar value items or a collection of a certain type of item. An example of this that I run into often is with box lots of books. If there is a table of boxes of books I usually try and search through them to see if there is any one book or box of books that is of great value, if I find such a box I will make my best bid and get that single box if possible or let other bidders thin the table with high enough bids to get the more valuable boxes that I may have overlooked. If I am interested in all the boxes at the right price I will try and make sure that every opening bid I have my hand up first, or if I notice the same buyers biding early and backing out I may jump the starting price and give a verbal opening bid of say $7 or $10 each time. I am waiting until the price is right for me, if I have no other bidders against me and the price is such that I am comfortable with it I will wave my hand in a line signaling that I am taking everything at that price. There might be a few boxes that I could have gotten cheaper, or possibly overpaid for but I will leave with books whereas if I had waited or just picked out a few boxes hoping the rest of the table gets auctioned off as one big lot than I might be leaving with nothing. There was an auction that I was at that had around one hundred mint in box Hess trucks, mostly newer models but from various years. I would be interested at any individual truck for $5 but I also would not complain with $7 a truck. The bid increments were $5,$7,$10,$15,$20 and so forth so in the first round the bidding went up to twenty dollars a pick and a few trucks were taken, next the bids stopped at ten dollars and ten or so trucks were taken. Looking around at the room I noticed a few potential dealers, which they are what would concern me as collectors at any auction generally only want specific items not mass quantities of items. The opening bid was five dollars and it paused there until the auctioneer said once, twice and I shouted six dollars! The auctioneer paused for a moment and then accepted my bid, which was not a typical amount but given that there were eighty five trucks left and the auctioneer had seen me purchase entire lots before went ahead. I won the bid and signaled that I was going to take the rest of the trucks, everyone cheered, mostly because it meant that we would be moving on to other items but also I am sure in part to the fact that I had just purchased eighty five trucks for over $500. The auctioneer was also so happy that he did not have to individually sell each truck gave me five for free which is common practice for buyers purchasing large quantities at a respectable price. I saved $30 from the auctioneer and I saved myself another $85 plus buyer's premium and tax by suggesting the $6 purchase price instead of the standard $7 which I was prepared to pay if need be. The bidder who was initially in for the opening $5 bid gave me a rather disturbing look and said he was going to buy the whole table and assumed I was just going to pick a few. I resold ten trucks on the spot for double what I paid to other upset bidders who did not get a shot and eventually sold the rest online for a profit of close to $1500.

Aggressive bidding is essential in any auction format, as fortune favors the bold. Routinely at the start of any estate or consignment auction I will try and make my presence known. If it is a large auction and there will be a lot of items I intend on bidding on than I may even overpay in the beginning of the auction for an item to show I can't be bullied and make bidders think twice before going against me later. If it is a bid for choice auction and there are five things in the row I want I might just go ahead and take all five to make an example. This can infuriate bidders and make them bid irrationally later on or force them to not be cheap and wait till the bidding gets low to get the items they want but instead bid fast and high early and take their items and get out of your way. If you are new to auctions or you're on a tight budget than I don't recommend taking chances with your money or over spending in any way. However if you do have some extra money to blow and your new to an auction, especially if you intend on returning to the auction in the future than it is not the worst idea making your presence known being aggressive early. I do mean within reason, if an item is worth $100, don't spend $150 on it because than you will just look like an idiot, but spending $80 in the beginning of a new unfamiliar auction might end up saving you money later on. Sometimes it is better to be feared than loved, and making a few enemies at first is a great way to make some friends later as you will get to know them as time goes on. It is an especially great feeling when people come up to me and essentially ask my permission to bid on items or to let them have an item. They are essentially in my pocket after that as I will expect them to return the favor.

## Storage Auctions

Having personally purchased in the hundreds of storage units in my days I will start this section off with a warning. I know many of you have seen the TV shows such as Storage Wars and Auction Hunters, these shows are mostly nothing more than good entertainment. They fail to show the reality of the business and all that it entails. They focus mainly on the successful purchases and valuable merchandise found inside. It is made to look so simple that anyone can do it but I have personally seen several people lose small fortunes trying to make it big in this business. I do not recommend the purchase of storage units for beginners! I cannot stress that enough. You need to have experience in selling large quantities of items as well as quickly on the fly establishing the potential resale value of items inside these units. You will also need a decent bankroll as many of these auctions will be CASH ONLY. If you feel like you have enough experience in sales and valuations of merchandise, or if you would like to disregard my advice about starting off with storage auctions I have made a quick checklist for you to get started.

<u>What you will need</u>

- Locks (preferably at least three key locks)

- Flashlight (the more powerful the better)

- Minimum $500 cash (I will explain why later)

- Work Gloves

- A truck/van or located a truck rental place

- A location to store the contents of the unit

- The will to be able to stop bidding when prices get outrageous

Now that you have everything off the checklist it is time to find some units to bid on! First, check your WhitePages, either online or print edition for storage related companies and give them a call. You will simply ask them when they are having auctions for their unpaid storage units, many places will fax you a list of the times and dates if they have multiple locations, or e-mail you a list. I would recommend trying some of the less popular companies in your area as the turnout to some of the less known ones may be drastically less. Most of the better known storage companies will have multiple auctions at one time and the simplest method is to show up for the first auction of the day and follow the auctioneer throughout the day to their various auctions. Another great method of finding when storage auctions will be held is by using one of my favorite websites auctionzip.com and it is totally free to use. You can search by region and date to find when auctions will be held.  You will want to ask or search on their websites what their policies and terms are for bidding. Many storage auctions will require that you remove all items within three days; others may be 24 hours to seven days. You will definitely want to find out what the payment methods accepted are, most will require for first time buyers that it is cash only however if you are a return customer (you have completed a sale and cleaned out the unit on time) they may be willing to accept credit cards, even checks in some rare cases if they are business checks. From a local storage company that I frequently purchased units at I was able to purchase on credit and they would send a bill to my company due within 30 days.

The types of storage auctions we would like to find and locate first are those that have primarily outside units.

Outside storage units are used a lot by businesses because they have the ability to bring their trucks in right up to the unit and load and unload them quickly and efficiently. In many cases they have access to the outdoor units virtually any time of day with an access gate code, this provides much flexibility. Outside units also tend to have a lot of larger items that would be otherwise very troublesome to transport into and out of an indoor online storage facility. You will commonly find small cars, motorcycles, small boats, automobile parts, office equipment, massive TVs, washers and dryers, furniture and many other large and heavy items in these outdoor units. If the storage company only has indoor units, make sure that it is a climate controls facility as ones that are not typically will not have the same concentration of high value contents in them.

The next thing we want to check is the area, I cannot stress this enough. I have storage units in some of the poorest inner city places before and other poor areas and the results were almost always the same. When I would be in a poor area buying units I would commonly find knock off merchandise, cheap brand names, literal trash, contents of the owners apartment, guns and weapons (only good part about these), drugs, roaches on more than one occasion and I even found contains of urine packaged in one which I assume was for passing drug tests. I have seen units that people were actually living inside of in these areas. I am not saying only go buy units in rich areas because that would not be a great idea as units in the richest of areas typically only have one or two units that month that were unpaid. I am suggesting that you find storage units that are located in decent locations with middle class families or areas with a lot of commercial and industrial businesses nearby.

Remember a lot of these storage companies offer incentives to get people to use their storage units, such as $1 for the first month is very common. These incentives will draw in a lot of the wrong crowd who will temporarily store items for the first month and pull out what they want at the end of the month and leave the rest which will then be auctioned off to the first sucker that thinks they are going to find gold. Many of the other victims of the $1 a month promotion will be those that could not afford to pay for the unit in the first place and at the end of the month they can't pay the bill and the unit is sold off. The items inside the unit will most likely be of little value. I will say this about units in poor areas; most of the units sold at auction will be very low priced. This is usually due to the contents found in these units but you may also be able to purchase three or four units for under a hundred bucks so if you are on a very tight budget and you are feeling up to the challenge of hauling away mostly junk feel free to take a few shots but don't say I did not warn you if you strike out! I can remember my very first storage auction that I went too, it was in the city of Baltimore and I purchased two units for a total of $25. I was extremely excited to go through it and make a fortune. For the most part I ended up finding mostly clothes which I donated and a lot of old food from someone's kitchen, but there was a large container of change which I took to CoinStar and pocketed $87 a decent stereo system, and other low grade electronics. It took me about six hours to haul everything back to my warehouse and another six to sort through everything. At the end of it all I ending up making about $650 but I had to rent a truck several times, first to haul the items back and again to haul them to the dump. It was a venture that took about 20 hours in total and after all expenses paid I only made about $20/hour. This kind of an experience would deter most first time buyers so let's talk about what we should be looking for when bidding on a unit.

When the lock on the storage unit is cut, which it should always be cut in the presence of the bidders, if it is not cut and has instead been replaced with one of the storage companies own beware the company and possibly insiders know already what is in the unit.

When the door opens – a few questions to ask yourself:

- Was this a commercial unit owned by a company? Or is it a personal unit? Business units might have inventory and quality throughout the unit.

- Does it look like the owner removed things of value and left garbage and did not pay his bill?

- Organization of the unit – is everything neatly placed or is everything just thrown into a pile?

- Are items put into trash bags? Usually a sign of what the owner thought of the contents inside or could afford.

- Is there a Washer & Dryer? Usually means someone put the contents of their home into during a move and will contain mostly housewares.

- Are there many large items you cannot fit in your truck/car/moving van?

- Are there items that you cannot lift by yourself?

- Is there any visible food or perishable items? Never a good sign.

What you should look for when the door opens:
- Look for neatly stacked plastic bins and cardboard boxes – avoid trash bags!

- Look for writing on the boxes/bins to possibly give some help of what is kept inside. ("Fine China", "Crystal", "Kitchen Items", "Clothes", "Books").

- A few items that you can properly value, if you know

the value of the items you can avoid overbidding

Another thing of note that can lead to huge profits and free inventory as well as point some coin in your pocket is storage unit clean outs. What I mean by this is that every storage company has to pay a company or an individual to clean out units that are not paid for and not sold at auction unless they are willing to do it themselves which is rarely the case. I have had deals with several different storage companies in the past and they pay usually anywhere from $50-$500 to clean out their units when they are not sold. Occasionally storage companies will hire a third party storage removal company to clean out the unit and transfer the responsibility of receiving payment for hauling to the owner of the unit. This is more so the case when an auction buyer wins a storage unit and does not clean it out, than they usually let the third party go after them for the fees.

This has happen to me personally once in the past, I won a unit full of TVs and electronics and I took out all of the stuff I wanted and then posted an ad on Craigslist to sell the remaining TVs. A buyer came and purchased the unit and I wrote a simple contract with this buyer to transfer the responsibility for cleaning out the unit to him. Sure enough he took a few TVs and left the rest in the storage unit, the storage company paid a company to clean it out and I got a bill for $700 for the service. Most storage companies will not allow you to transfer ownership and responsibility of cleaning out a unit to anyone else; I would advise asking the company about it if you are planning on attempting this. I would have the legal authority to sue the buyer of my contract to clean out the unit since he was in breach, and then the hauling company could sue me for their charges and so forth but nothing ever came of it either way.

## A few buying strategies for longer term higher profits from storage auctions, estate sales & auctions, yard sales, thrift stores, etc:

There are three different strategies that can be used for buying and holding inventory that you buy from estate sales, estate auctions, business liquidations, thrift stores, yard sales, storage auction (only if you have a lot of storage space). Typically this is how I do business now that I don't have to worry about my income anymore.

Strategy one is very basic and simple and very short term. For a two week period I buy inventory, I focus completely on buying only. This is important because if you go buy inventory at an auction or where ever and then list it and then go to another auction than list it, etc you will end up having to ship products, list products and buy products at the same time and it becomes overwhelming if you are handling any type of volume. In this first strategy I take out anywhere from $5000-$10000 cash. I make a list of every estate sale, auction, storage auction, business liquidation and I like to make a note of thrift stores and yard sales at the end of the two week period if I still need more inventory, or if I have money left over. I buy and buy until I run out of my reserved cash and store my entire inventory at my location. Than for the next week I take pictures, test items, clean them, fix them and whatever else is needed, by the end of the week I will have listed the items at auction or on a fast flipping marketplace (usually over a hundred items). After that I can focus on shipping items only for the next two weeks as they end from auctions. Items that don't sell at auction go in one of my stores. This way I don't have to worry about shipping items everyday and buying items every week. Typically there is about a 60 turnover from start to finish selling everything, but I can gross $30k+ from $10k spending on inventory at these venues.

The second strategy that I use involves me keeping at least $30k worth of inventory throughout my E-Commerce sites, eBay and Amazon stores, etc. When my inventory drops to about half I go out and make sure I buy $15k worth of resell able inventory. I am currently exercising this style now because I don't have time for much else. I only have to work a few days a month buying items and selling items but I can make a few hundred dollars an hour doing so. I don't have to worry about selling items for less than they are worth at an auction site, by listing them in the stores I can maximum value for all of my items or I simply don't sell them. If I still have a massive amount of inventory after a few months only then will I liquidate them.

The last strategy that I do is from August until November I only buy inventory, I usually rely on my store sales from older inventory to carry me until November in sales. The purpose here is to hit the biggest and highest return sales period of the year – CHRISTMAS! Customers start buying like wild maniacs in November so if you have been stock piling inventory until then you will get the best return on your money in most cases unless you have a lot of seasonal only items.

Once again this style of selling is really only suited for those selling as a hobby or with reserve capital to be able to go sustained periods without an income and heavy spending.

# Drop Shipping

This may be the most sought after method of sales for new sellers in the online world, but it can also be the most difficult and least profitable to maintain. First let me explain what drop shipping is for those who do not already know. Drop shipping is the process of selling an item that you do not physically have in your procession, when the item sells you place an order for that product with the drop shipping distributor and have them ship the item to your customer directly. If you have an account with the distributor and say you can buy item B for $50 and you can sell it for $75 to a customer, you pocket the difference minus any fees that are involved. Some drop shippers will charge a handling fee for this service, usually in the range of $1.50 to $4.00 depending on the item and business. No legitimate drop shipping company will charge you a fee to sign up, this is a scam! This is also done by third party drop shippers, they pose as the source of the inventory but they really have no products of their own and simply use accounts with other drop ship companies. These fake drop shippers will slightly mark up the cost and squeeze out a little more profit from their customers who think they are buying direct. Another thing you may need to consider if drop shipping is something you are considering pursuing is to register for an EIN which is known as an employer identification number also known as a federal tax id through the IRS. You may also need to have a reseller id for some companies, this is also known as a sales and use tax certificate and it is used to pay local state taxes on sales but it is usually not asked for. With the reseller id you can purchase items and not have to pay tax on the purchases until you sell the inventory and you pay taxes on your earnings. You will have to check your local state government website to find links to apply for this as it varies from state to state.

There is a lot of competition amongst sellers listing drop ship items so the biggest key to success that I have found through the years of selling drop ship goods is to pick a niche product line and focus on selling that type of product at first and then expanding. Many people new to drop shipping do not understand market research, product demand and availability or pricing for that matter. These people rush into it looking for the most popular products they can think of that sell for the highest prices. Such sellers try and sell Xbox 360's, iPads, iPods, HDTVs, Laptops and other popular products. Why they won't be successful is because there is an enormous amount of other sellers trying to sell the same types of products and the few legitimate drop shippers that carry these products are either drop shipping them directly from the manufacturer or buying them wholesale from the manufacturer and reselling them to you so you can sell the products for them. Unless you have hundreds of thousands of dollars in free cash you will not be able to setup a drop shipping account with a manufacturer such as Apple, Sony, Microsoft, etc as they are only interested in the big sellers, not someone selling products one at a time. I remember when I first started drop shipping and I wanted to sell the original Microsoft Xbox which had just come out and after hours of searching around I found a drop shipper that carried this product in stock. The MSRP for the XBOX at the time was $200, the drop shipper was offering the XBOX for $175 for an individual sale and $172 for a purchase of ten and a low of $170 for more than twenty. As you can see this does not leave hardly any room for profit, especially if you were trying to sell it on a site like eBay or Amazon because the fees alone will basically make you break even. I did manage to make a small profit selling twenty of the XBOX's drop shipped to a business associate of mine who in turn resold them locally for a small profit as well. The point of this run down is that it is very hard to make a lot of money if you are trying to sell an extremely popular product that you have virtually no profit margin on.

You need to be the owner of a store or a wholesaler with massive cash reserves to drop ship the product directly from the manufacturer.

Drop shipping is very popular online and offline, just think about how many times you have gone to your mail box and pulled out catalogs filled with products that you can buy. These products are almost always being drop shipped directly to you when you make a purchase. These catalog mailing companies usually have little to no physical inventory. They usually buy leads from companies who sell your information to them, typically if you have purchased similar products else ware and supplied your personal information, it may be at risk. Have you ever gone to a mattress or furniture showroom and made a purchase? Usually these types of companies only keep a display model of each product they are selling and you cannot purchase and take home the product that day, it is instead delivered to you at a later date. This is how these types of company keep their inventory space to a minimum and don't lose out on products that do not sell, especially when they are very costly to purchase in the first place.

Another very successful and popular technique for drop shipping is by selling a product at cost or even losing money on the sale at an online auction. This is done by companies and individuals that have their own websites and by selling an item to you cheaper than anyone else they hope to get your future business. They will also have your personal information after you purchase the item, they also may require you to complete the check out procedure through their own checkout system on their website. This essentially makes you a customer of their website and they will send you e-mail newsletters, catalogs in the mail, coupons and even resell your information to other companies.

An emerging trend in the drop ship business is to use private label drop shipping, in which a manufacturer produces a custom item for a retailer and drop ships it. The range of private label drop shipped items varies from simple key chains and t-shirts with custom logos or pictures to customized formulations for vitamins and nutritional supplements.

If you are going to venture into drop shipping the best place to start is your own personal website, there are many hosting providers that will set you up with your own personal E-Commerce website now for a few bucks. There are many great free software packages you can download and be up and running in minutes, one such package is OSCommerce and it is a fully featured shopping cart solution. Another package which can be installed free and automatically if you purchase a hosting account is called Zen Cart with most hosting providers. You will also want to have a template designed or purchase a custom made template for your website so it does not look basic and unprofessional if you do not have knowledge of web design. Do not be fooled into purchasing a pre built website filled with products ready to sell that you will just automatically start selling them. If you are trying to sell products on your website you will need to do some marketing and advertising. The simplest and easiest starting point is to sign up with Google Adwords, you should get a free advertising credit if you sign up with Godaddy to purchase your domain name and hosting, currently they offer $100 in advertising on Facebook and Google to new customers which more than pays for any domain and hosting costs you just incurred.

eBay and Amazon can be a great place to sell drop shipped goods but you need to make sure that you are doing proper market research, especially if you plan on listing items at auction. If you list a bunch of products starting out at .99 cents and they only get one bid and sell at that price you will either be forced to drop ship your product to the customer at a potential loss or cancel the transaction, if you have to cancel to many transactions you will most likely receive many negative feedbacks and may be kicked off the site you were selling on. If you are using eBay to sell drop shipped goods I suggest you open up a ProStore and an eBay store as well as a personal website to try and back sell items to your customers. You will want to use my drop ship calculator located in your members section of ereselling.com. Drop shipping profitably is all about the numbers, by using the calculator you can quickly estimate potential profits or losses of selling an item at an online auction, Amazon, your personal website payment processing charges and other fees you may incur in the sale of a product.

Now you will need to locate some products that you are interested in selling and the companies that are available that offer drop shipping. I have provided many verified and personally used drop shipping companies in your members section of the eReselling.com website, but I will not be redistributing lists that other companies have worked very hard to maintain and create. The best place for you to locate drop shipping companies is hands down World Wide Brands that I have used since 2002 and it offers the biggest list of verified drop shippers with over 8,000 companies currently in their database, they are the easiest to use and most reliable company I have come across. You can search for products that you would like to sell and their database will match the products to the company and you can apply to setup your account with the drop shipper directly through the World Wide Brands website. The benefit of this is that you can apply to hundreds of companies in a matter of minutes, all your information is stored in your profile and forwarded to the drop shippers you are applying too. You will not have to visit each company individually and fill out hundreds of forms to setup accounts. When I had my corporation and sold massive amounts of drop shipped products we found all of drop shippers here, they do not get any commission for referring customers or incentives. All drop shippers listed in their directory are constantly updated and removed if inactive.

They are also listed on the eBay website as a verified third party solutions provider. My company iNetDirectSales, Inc also owned a wholesale/drop ship packaging company that made specially crafted foam packaging material and we were listed on World Wide Brands directory and I can assure you we had sign ups everyday and I never paid a penny to be listed in their directory and they did not pay us either.

There are some down sides to drop shipping you need to be aware of. You may encounter back ordering when you place a shipment request with the distributor or wholesaling drop ship company, but the product is sold out. Back ordering may be accompanied by a long wait for a shipment while the wholesaler waits for new products, which may reflect badly on the retailer. A good wholesaler will keep retailers updated, but it is the business owner's job to be aware of the quantities that the wholesaler has available.

My personal successes from drop shipping did not happen immediately, I signed up with about thirty companies which was way to many and picked a few products from each company to sell which made it very difficult when the time came to place successful orders and find the corresponding company with the product. Trying out many different companies is not a bad idea, but do not overwhelm yourself with too much at once. Make sure you keep track of the item numbers or product IDs of the items you are attempting to drop ship. Use an excel spreadsheet, database or if your selling on eBay use the "notes" feature in Turbo Lister or on the eBay listing tool too include the company the item is being drop shipped from, the item number and especially the quantity they have on hand if available. Make sure when products you have listed on your website, eBay and Amazon and other locations become unavailable or out of stock that you update your inventory. If you are going to be listing a large quantity of products make sure you check on them daily. There are many drop shippers that will offer you a daily updated spreadsheet, RSS feed or FTP link to download their current inventory. If you have a website, there are many shopping carts available that will allow you to upload the inventory file and automatically update the inventory you have listed on your website with the appropriate quantities.

Drop shipping can also be used as a last resort mechanism to save face with a customer who has purchased an item you have lost for example. I have had to use this method many times on Amazon, a customer purchases a book that I cannot locate or have sold on another site and forgot to update my inventory. I will locate the product somewhere else online or use the Amazon listing that the customer purchased the product from and purchase the same item from the next seller who has this book in the same condition I was listing mine for. Typically in doing so I will take a slight loss on the sale but I will avoid canceling the listing on Amazon and upsetting a customer by not delivering the product that was purchased. If you have to cancel over 2% of your orders on Amazon you will receive a warning and then you will be suspended. This has happened to me before, I went on vacation and forgot to set my store status to "On Vacation" and I received five orders the first night and realized that I would not return in time to meet Amazon's required shipping time so I canceled every order and a week later my account was suspended for doing so. There is another less common practice seen by some very sneaky drop shippers on Amazon. This process involves an Amazon seller having a very high feedback rating and reputation and using it to resell other Amazon sellers products. While that may have sounded a bit confusing, I assure you it was meant to be. Basically in order to pull this off an Amazon seller will need software to track and update current prices of products listed on the site with the current price they are selling the item for in their inventory. An example of this if I am the seller trying to profit from this system, I find a product that is rather valuable and has a high sell through rate or a product in which only one or two other sellers are selling that I have a higher feedback rating or better rating than. They are listing product A for $1000, I will list the same product for $1100 and hope the customer chooses me over the other sellers. If they do so, I purchase the product from the other seller who was selling it for $100 and have them ship the item to the customer, I profit the difference without having to have a product of my own to sell. In order to pull this off you would need a way to track the prices and the sellers of an item because if they raise the price to close to yours or they sell their product first you could be in for a world of trouble. This type of selling was documented by a weird case that happened in 2010 where a book with an MSRP of $25 ended up being listed on the Amazon website for over one million dollars by two sellers. Each seller was trying to use the drop ship method described above but when one seller would raise the price it triggered the other seller's software to in turn raise their price and eventually the price reached one million dollars and Amazon was notified of this and made the sellers correct their prices.

Finding true companies that will drop ship for you has become a lot easier in recent years, especially with the ever growing popularity of drop shipping. The problem with locating the companies has to do with the enormous amount of companies and scam artists trying to sell wholesale list and dropship list and it is very hard to sort through and find real companies in the mix if you are using search engines. Another problem with locating them on search engines is that they are Business-to-Business (B2B) supplies and their sites do not usually get the same amount of traffic or have enough links pointing to them to rank high in the search engines. You may have to search deep in the search engines but you can pull out legit companies this way. Another way to find drop shipping companies is to sign up for Alibaba.com and locate the wholesalers of merchandise your interested in and find out if they have a drop shipping program, many of them certainly will. If you are not willing to search for legit drop ship companies I suggest you sign up for WorldWideBrands.com you won't be disappointed.

As a final thought on drop shipping profitably, especially if you are using online auctions you should create some variations of the keywords in your listing title and try listing a small amount of products at a time to find out which ones are successful. When you find a product that sells at a very high and profitable sell through rate you can simply relist it over and over, eventually your product line will grow as you add in new products and keep selling proven profitable ones. There was a time back in 2005 when I could list 100 products everyday at auction profitably with a single click of eBay's Turbo Lister program. You can do the same, it just takes time and patience and you can make as much money as you desire if you never give up.

**Wholesale Importing & Reselling**

**Accounts to create:**
- **ALIBABA.COM** – Wholesale Supplier & Distributor

  Marketplace

- **TRADEKEY.COM** - Wholesale Supplier & Distributor

  Marketplace

- **LIQUIDATION.COM** – Liquidation Inventory Buying

**Optional accounts to create:**
- **ALERT PAY.COM** – (FREE) To send money

  Internationally (PayPal not always accepted)

- **MONEY BOOKERS.COM** – (FREE) Another Payment

  Alternative to PayPal and AlertPay

- **World Wide Brands.com** – Drop Ship / Wholesale

  Directory Site (Amazing – Just not free!)

Many of the same companies that offer drop shipping services will also provide wholesale accounts and vice versus. Typically wholesale rates will be from 50-60% off retail but this varies between product lines, quantities and middlemen involved. The key here is that we are getting as many middlemen out of the way as possible and getting the lowest price we can to ensure that our margins are not to squeezed. Wholesale purchases and accounts may be hard to establish with popular name brands such as Nintendo or Sony without massive amounts of capital. Sometimes you will also need a reseller id, tax id and other requirements in order to create an account, as well as references and banking information. This will usually not be the case if we are establishing accounts with international companies outside of your own, although you may want to check your local laws for importing fees, certifications and taxes. If your heart is set on selling Nintendo Wii game systems per say there are plenty of other options, you can find a distributor or reseller in your country or area and establish an account with them. This will not give you the lowest possible rate, as you will have to pay them a handling fee and marked up price but you will still have your product.

There are some great sites available to us where we can find wholesale suppliers, manufacturers and distributors. Three sites that you definitely want to check out and make accounts with are **ALIBABA** and **TRADEKEY** and **LIQUIDATION**. These will be your best friends if you're just getting started; they have searchable directories for products and companies. You can find suppliers worldwide and establish accounts in a matter of minutes.

One of the biggest problems you will face is counterfeit goods, they are being sold everywhere! Alibaba especially is a haven for knock off goods even though they strictly prohibit them. When you find a supplier you are happy with and you like their prices and product line contact them and request a sample before you make your order. If a supplier is not willing to provide you with a sample item then you should be very skeptical and my advice would be to pass on them.

There are certainly some gray areas, or at least shades of gray with selling items that come from wholesalers in countries like China. It is easy to overlook the fact that a huge portion of the items made in China are created by children in sweat shops when the prices are so good and you are only thinking about dollar signs. The issue is that the suppliers will usually not reveal information about their workforce or deny anything unethical so it really is up to you to decide if you want to do business in a location that does not have strict labor laws. Another issue is the integrity of items that you are importing, for instance many, many years ago when I was just starting out and very naive I wanted to sell NFL Jerseys and Lacoste shirts. I found a company on Alibaba that was selling "Authentic NFL Jerseys" and another company selling "Authentic 100% Mother of Pearl Lacoste Polo Shirts". I ordered $200 worth of NFL Jerseys and $200 of Lacoste shirts for resale. I got the jerseys and shirts and they looked great, and I was quick to slap them on eBay and sell them to my friends. I had 20 Lacoste shirts and 10 jerseys and I sold them all in about a week for a $600 profit! I quickly reinvested the money back into jerseys and shirts and flipped the shirts and jerseys again and again until I had several thousand dollars worth of jerseys and shirts in my possession. It wasn't until two months later did I find out they were NOT authentic, they were just very well made knock offs. I had a customer of each of the items complain and return the items saying they were fake and when I investigated further I was able to confirm they were "knock offs" that I was selling as authentic. I felt horrible, but this practice is done every day by thousands of sellers online, and no that does not make it ok. Morally I was not ok with selling the remainder of items I had in stock as authentic so I listed them online and described them just as they were as very well made authentic style items and I was able to sell them all with no problem and 100% positive feedback but for less money, about double what I paid. I also sold them locally to a lot of my friends and colleagues by telling them exactly what they were "This is a knock off jersey; give me $40 for it – true authentic jerseys sell for $250". It was a no brainer and they knew exactly what they were getting for the money, no moral issues, no lying and everyone is happy. I still do this today, but I don't sell them online, people ask me to buy them wholesale from China and I help them out and I do it for just about cost these days.

## Dumpsters, Free Pickup Items, Free Books

This will be beyond the majority of the readers but I

feel that it can still be educational and profitable for those who are willing to dig deep for that extra income. Personally there was a time in my life where I was so broke and in debt that I would do anything for money, that is what it will take for you to consider this idea for the most part. Most of the inventory that I have gotten from dumpsters has been by accident. I am not now, nor have I ever been a dumpster diver, there is no amount of money that will allow me to forfeit my pride and climb into a dumpster to look for something to sell. Now that I have gotten that out of the way, I will open the side door of a dumpster that I know has only cardboard boxes in it for the most part and pull out boxes to use for shipping. I live near a large shopping center that has a Barnes & Noble, Target, Hallmark, Old Navy, Blockbuster, Dunkin Donuts and not too far away are a few movie theatres which have some goodies in them. All of these stores have dumpsters behind them that they fill with boxes and packaging material such as bubble wrap and shrink wrap which I will drive by and fill up my vehicle with. I have saved literally over $10,000 in packaging this way, hands down no questions asked.

While pulling boxes out of the dumpster sometimes I notice a box full of items. This happens more often than I would like to see as I do not like to route around in a dumpster even if it is done remotely. When I say remotely I mean that I use a very long pole with a hook on the end to pull out boxes. I will also use a flashlight sometimes if it is dark out and I am worried about touching something I don't want to.

I will get straight to the point and share some examples of what I have found in dumpsters as this subject is one I don't want to spend an unnecessary amount of time on. From the Barnes & Noble dumpster once a month they trash about ten large boxes of books that have been on their shelves for too long. I always figured they would be returned to the publisher but I guess under certain circumstances they purchase books outright. I will pull out two, maybe three boxes and take them with me as I have an issue with maintaining my pride. Generally there are about thirty books in each box, they are ranging from children's books to doctors manuals. For a quick flip I list them on Amazon, I will usually make anywhere from $100-$300 on the boxes I pull out which is all profit. I once pulled out a box of books that were all doctors manuals for different types of surgery procedures and I sold one box for over $500.

At the local Blockbuster I would typically find bags full of empty DVD cases. These would typically be new releases that they have maybe fifty copies of and a few months later not be in need of such a quantity and would use a machine to destroy the contents of the DVD but leave the case and movie cover in perfect condition. Each bag might contain a hundred DVD cases in it and I would pull a bag or two depending on what mood I was in. 200 DVD cases can easily be broken down into smaller lots of say 50 cases for $25. This means while you are getting boxes you just pocketed $100 profit for doing nothing more than removing a bag of cases, taking a picture, listing and shipping them which does not take long at all. The other types of items I have frequently pulled out from Blockbuster are new life size standee and movie posters from the same new releases as the DVD cases that were not sold during the promotion period. These can easily be flipped for $20-$50 or more each if the movie is of great popularity.

The Hallmark dumpster is one that I like to visit for boxes as I can find every size imaginable on a daily basis. They also seem to discard some of the craziest inventory. For starters I once pulled out a commercial poster media large format printer and sold it as for parts or repair for $400. Routinely they discard inventory after every holiday and you can find boxes of perfectly good Yankee Candles, ornaments, decorations and other seasonal inventory that went unsold. They also discard items that have small defects, which seems like it should be in the trash but items of high value with small defects still have good market value. I will give you a quick example of one such find, I pulled out two very large boxes that were filled with close to fifty different types of Vera Bradley purses, handbags, clutches and women's accessories. Each item had a very small defect such as a very small stain, hole or tear on it. I listed the items exactly in the condition they were in as five separate wholesale lots; I made over $500 from about a solid hours work.

The other stores I mentioned are great for finding boxes, I have never really found much else in their dumpsters. The movie theatre however is a different story all together. When a new movie is released the theatre is sent very large standees and posters as well as promotional material for the movie. The theatre will put these items on display before and during the movie release. When the movie leaves the theatre so do the posters and standees. Sometimes the employees of the theatre will get to take certain pieces home, I know this because my brother used to work at the movie theatre and would bring me home all sorts of items to sell. Other times the movie theatre will be contractually obligated to return the promotional materials to the movie studio. The third scenario is where we cash in, they put these materials in their dumpster. I am not talking about the small standees and posters you may find at Blockbuster, I am talking huge wall sized and parade sized cardboard, plastic and carbon fiber decorations and figures. I sold one such Spiderman figure for over $400, Marge Simpson for several hundred, the whole set sold on eBay for over $3,000!

The other possible solution for dumpsters is to wait until the end of a college semester and visit a college campus. I have not personally done this, but I have been at several colleges to help friends and family move out and into college. College students that are done for the semester will throw away just about everything they are too lazy to haul back home. If they are traveling and going to school abroad than they will leave just about everything they purchased during the semester. I warn you however you may have some competition if you are looking to cash in using this method as there may be other dumpster divers who will beat you to it. A possible solution would be to post flyers on the bulletin boards of the dorm room areas a few weeks before students move out and offer them a consignment deal, or maybe even better yet you can offer to haul away their possessions free of charge or a small fee.

I hope I have clarified my position on dumpster inventory, as I will not by any means promote or encourage people to jump into their neighborhood dumpsters in search of treasures that other people have thrown away. If you are inclined to do such I wish you the best of luck but make sure you stay away from needles and say hi to the rats for me.

It has been several years since I have used dumpsters as a source of inventory but over a two year period that I frequented them for boxes I pulled out and sold over $5000 worth of items which was basically free money. If you have similar stores in your area than I am sure you can expect to find the same types of items. This section was meant to make you think outside the box and about the businesses near you to find possible opportunities to "double dip". Double dipping in this sense would mean that we are locating a free source of boxes and packaging materials and at the same time finding free inventory to sell. This can be a life saving venture for those in dire need of money. I would much rather see someone pulling out inventory from a dumpster than standing on a street corner begging other people to give them their hard earned money because they don't know how to find a job or make money with nothing. In fact I would encourage you to hand them a copy of my book before giving them anything they did not earn.

Another way to get yourself free inventory is to check out sites like Craigslist and other classified listings, search for "free" or "free you haul" and similar listings. You will find many people moving or trying to clear up space in their garages and basements that will literally give away things if you come and pick them up! You can also find a lot of trades and bartering available.

Another simple way to stock up on inventory is look for book exchanges like BookThing.org that literally have a maximum give away of up to 150,000 books per person per visit! There are a lot of these types of free book non-profit companies available. The books are stamped usually as "Free book" or "Not for resale" but you can use your own judgment. Personally I sell these types of books only when I have donated to them at least ten times as many books as I take. You can also call your local library; they donate and sometimes give away old books that have been in use.

Use these generally examples to expand the amount of items you can get free and the different types as there are many ways you can make money without spending money if you just use your head!

# Chapter 4 – Creating a physical Product or Selling a Service

Do you have a great idea for a product? Think you can improve on an existing product or make it cheaper? Are you good with your hands or know someone that is? Do you have a particular skill that you can provide customers a service with? If you answered no to the above questions you may want to skip this chapter, otherwise buckle up and get ready to make something!

First I will discuss some products and services that I have made or paid someone or a company to create for me and resell to help you get a better understanding of the unlimited possibilities. When I first started selling online and on eBay I had lost my license and was trapped in my room for a lot of the time which got me thinking about ways I could make some money. In the early 2000's the internet connections were not as fast as they are today for the most part for home users so creating a product and e-mailing or having it digitally delivered was not as feasible as it is today. I was very big into cars at this time and spent a lot of time at the local drag strip and some underground street races and had recorded a bunch of footage. I decided to combine all of the footage I had and some additional footage I collected (non-copyrighted) and compiled a VCD (Video CD) and later onto DVD format that could be watched with ease. I also purchased some DVD sticky labels and printed out a bunch of labels with pictures of my favorite car, the Mazda RX-7. I started listing five copies of my CD/DVD on eBay with a great listing featuring pictures of some of the cars on the CD/DVD, small video clips people could download to preview. Over the next three weeks selling my videos I made a profit of about $500 – they were selling like hotcakes! I had a buy it now for $14.99 and $9.99 auction price. The sell through rate was between 25-35% meaning I could list a ton of listings at various times throughout the day and still make a profit, the ones that did not sell the first time I could relist and if they sold the second time I would be refunded my original insertion fee.

With the success of my first product I was curious what else I could put on a CD or DVD and sell. Sticking with my love of cars and the RX-7 I did some searching and found some non-copyright protected repair and maintenance manuals for each year that the car was made. The manuals took up a lot of hard drive space so e-mailing them was not an option. I formatted the manuals onto a CD so that a computer could easily open and read the data. My second product was born, I created a variation of about five different listings to attract buyers for each generation of RX-7 (there were three). The manuals were a success but the sell through rate was considerable lower than the racing DVD coming in between 10-20%. The cost to list each CD on eBay back then was 35 cents so listing ten of them meant $3.50 in fees. I was able to sell the CDs for $10-$20 as there was nobody else selling them on eBay which meant I controlled the market. I would list 70 of them a week, ten everyday at different times meaning my listing fees were around $25 a week, but actually a bit less considering the listings that did not sell the first time I would relist and be refunded my original listing fee if the sale was successful. I don't want to get to technical into the numbers for the purpose of this section but basically with the average sell through rate and average sales price in a given week I was averaging around $160 a week in sales. I charged a very low shipping and handling fee but it was enough to cover the cost of my final value fees and shipment. Minus the cost of the disc, labels and listing fees I would see an average profit of around $100 a week from this product line. I spent a weekend burning hundreds of these CDs and the previous racing CDs so that when a sale came in it was already packaged and ready to go putting my eBay sales on virtual auto pilot.

Next I was able to find out a way for an owner of a Honda, Acura, Mazda, Toyota and a few other makers of cars to increase the horsepower of their vehicle. The technique was taught to me by one of my friends who was a mechanic and it involved installing a ten cent resistor onto the vehicles ignition crank sensor if my memory serves me correctly. This was called a timing advance mod. As to avoid being sued I printed up a detailed letter that would protect me from any liability if any damage were to be done to the vehicle it was installed on. I also printed up a two page installation manual for installing the resistor. When the sale was complete I would fold up both the non-liability form and manual with the resistor and mail it in an envelope to the customer. This cost me a stamp to send out and about 20 cents in materials to make. I had no trouble selling this product for $20 a pop on eBay and would use about twenty different variations of listings for different makes and models of vehicles it would work on. I sold about three hundred of these until finally someone had a problem with the mod and threatened to sue me so I discontinued selling this product. Also when you have a great idea other people will try and steal it, at first I was selling these timing advance mods at an average of a 50% sell through. A few months later it dropped to about 15% and I could not understand why until I checked eBay listings at auction and saw that the market had become flooded with the same product I was selling and the sellers were just copying my listing and idea. I looked a bit deep and I noticed one of the sellers that were listing this product was a former buyer of my product and had just relisted it. Listing a product that can be easily recreated and resold can be a serious problem and there is often times little to nothing you can do about it.

Not being great with my hands or crafting I was searching for something simple to create and resell. I was thinking about popular games that people like to play, especially outdoor games and it hit me! Cornhole was a game that was growing in popularity. I saw it being played at tailgates, family gatherings, backyards, bars and just about anywhere outside people could. I found a simple manual to build a regulation sized Cornhole set online and with the help of two of my cousins we built our first set. Materials cost about $30 a set with the wood we used and cloth for the bags, we used many variations and different schematics and were eventually able to get the cost to around $20 for the standard set and $60 for premium which included a full painting. The Cornhole sets that were sold on eBay were for around $100 and up to $200 if we special painted the boards with say the colors of a buyers favorite team. We had more orders than we could fill for this project and demand for these types of games is usually through the rough during the summer and Christmas season. This product is best sold locally, but can also be sold on sites like eBay and shipped. To sell a product such as this one I recommend listing it on the following sites:

- Craigslist.org (free)

- Etsy.com (Great for homemade products)

- eBay classified listings (free)

- eBay Store (local pickup is easiest)

- Personal website

# 55 Items that you can make and sell online!

1. **Cornhole Sets.** This is one of the hottest games ever created for tailgating, BBQ's and family fun yet they can be made by anyone!
2. **Hand painted plates & cups.** Even if you can't make cups, you can paint them!
3. **Paintings and drawings.** Though you probably won't get high-end prices for paintings, you can still get decent prices from Etsy.
4. **Sunflower Seeds & Pumpkin Seeds.** Very simple and cheap to produce, bake these goodies up and add some seasonings and you got yourself a healthy resalable snack!
5. **Handmade handbags.** Make a handbag out of interesting materials. Go for the classy or artsy look.
6. **Creative wallets**. Make your own wallets with special designs.
7. **Knitted kids shoes.** Knit warm and snuggly shoes for kids.
8. **Home printed T-shirts.** A great way to express your sense of style.
9. **Hand sewn clothing**. You can even offer tailoring if they have specific measurements.
10. **Crochet gloves.** Hand-crocheted gloves often feel warmer and cozier than factory made.
11. **Crochet hats.** Add a unique design to give it some flair.
12. **Handmade sandals.** Sandals are easy to make and offer a lot of room for creativity.
13. **Decorated dolls.** Doll collectors and kids love creative designs.
14. **Creative glass decorations.** If you're into glass art, this is a fantastic way to make some money.
15. **Hand sewn pillow cases.** Buy some gorgeous fabrics from your local fabric store, sew it into a pillow's shape and list it on Etsy. Perfect for beginners!

16. **Hand sewn tissue boxes**. Be sure to put some stiffer material inside so it keeps the shape.

17. **Handmade silver jewelry.** One of the higher priced items on Etsy, giving you some room for markup.

18. **Hand knit coffee cup holders.** Who wouldn't want to slip their daily cup of coffee into a hand-knit cup holder?

19. **Hand stamped guitar picks.** Offer to engrave or burn in names, bands or slogans into guitar picks.

20. **Hand carved guitar picks.** Carve guitar picks by hand using beautiful wood as a base.

21. **Homemade chocolate.** If it tastes great, you'll probably get repeat sales.

22. **Natural dried fruits.** Easy to make with a dehydrator.

23. **Hand carved chess set.** These can go for a lot of money (though they're also a lot of work.)

24. **Handmade wooden pen.** A gentlemen's classic.

25. **Handmade kaleidoscopes.** Some wood and a few pieces of glass can produce a world of magic.

26. **Personalized or handmade instruments (guitars, flutes, drums.)** A very specialized skill.

27. **Shell jewelry**. If you live near a beach, go find the most elegant shells you can and craft jewelry from them.

28. **Leather bracelets**. Learning to make buckles or cut leather isn't difficult; the trick is developing an eye for what kind of bracelets people want.

29. **Custom fitted corsets.** For women with more gothic or vintage tastes, this is more of a low-volume high-margin product.

30. **Geek paraphernalia.** Video game art and school of wizardry wands generate quite a few sales, believe it or not.

31. **Handmade watches (or watch bands.)** Make someone a custom watch with a unique design. If you don't know how to make watches, just buy the watch piece and custom design the wristband.

32. **Decorated water bottles.** Give your customers the joy of going hiking or to yoga with a unique and creative water

bottle.

33. **Scented candles.** Make unique scents they can't find in stores.

34. **Woodwick candles.** Instead of using a nylon wick, put wood in the middle instead. It burns longer and releases more fragrance. A very niche product.

35. **Strangely shaped soaps (sword, hands, angels.)** Gives the bathroom a touch of personality.

36. **Books you wrote.** If you're not officially published, try selling a few books on Etsy.

37. **Handmade bookmarks.** Just about anyone can make bookmarks. How well they'll sell depends entirely on your design.

38. **Animal-free bath products.** Mix your own soap, shampoo or toothpaste to cater to the vegan crowd.

39. **Headbands.** Knit, sew or crochet headbands.

40. **Hair clips.** Though small in size, they offer infinite possibilities in design. Should you add a small glass bird? Perhaps a flower?

41. **Decorated pocket mirrors.** A touch of class never hurts when someone needs to do their makeup in public.

42. **Bras and lingerie.**

43. **Homemade perfume or cologne**. Create better scents with fewer chemicals than commercial varieties.

44. **Creative key chains**. Perhaps add a Lego piece for geeks or a dinosaur's tooth for the wealthy.

45. **Rings**. You can cater to just about any audience with rings.

46. **Earrings.** First think about who your audience is. Then think about what they want. (Classy? Unique? Sexy? Conversation starters?) Start your design with that in mind.

47. **Pendants and necklaces.** Have an interesting center piece for a necklace? Start with the pendant, then the necklace.

48. **Creative belts.** Either make the belt from scratch, or buy plainer belts and make them more stylish.

49. **Assorted candy box.** If you have a great taste for sweets, perhaps others would like your selections as well.

50. **Carvings.** Wealthier clients will love having hand carved products to decorate their homes with.

51. **Ladder Toss.** This is an extremely fun game to play that is growing in popularity and easy to make and sell!

52. **Bird houses.** This is an extremely easy thing to make if you have some basic wood cutting and carving tools, be crafty and sand and paint them.

53. **Totem Poles & Wooden Figures.** These can be sold for huge dollar amounts, this will take some skills and wood working tools but the profits can be huge!

54. **Crochet & Knitting.** If your good with your hands and you can make a quilt or blanket – go for it!

55. **Packaging Materials.** This might seem to complicated but if you have access to foam, cardboard, plastics than you might have some huge profits awaiting. We made a shipping product out of foam cut outs and sold them for huge profits – they would have been thrown away otherwise!

# Chapter 5 –How to Sell

You should understand by now exactly where you can sell items, how to find items to sell and how to make your own products so now it is time to learn a few tricks for selling them successfully and better than your competition.

Always have batteries on hand if you are buying and selling anything used and electronic. It would be a good idea to keep at least a pack or have rechargeable batteries of each of the common types such as AAA, AA, D and C. Believe me you will need to use each of them. If you are at an auction, yard sale, thrift store don't be scared to pop in some batteries and plug up some items to a power outlet before you make a bid or purchase! Always check battery compartments on any item before you buy it to make sure there is no corrosion or damage, a lot of people leave batteries in items and forget about them and over time they will destroy the device.

Make sure that your product is the same product that you think it is. That may seem like common sense but if you are selling a lot of items at once and you don't know much about the items you are selling it may be easy to associate your product with one you have seen elsewhere. You may see an antique or vintage item and your product may look virtually the same but it could be a reproduction or just a newer model of the same product. If you try selling this product as an antique and it's not your reputation may be at stake.

Always clean your products up and make them look presentable. Take a lot at a product your trying to sell and ask yourself if you would buy it looking in the current condition it is in. Selling a cleaned up collectible versus a dirt and dust covered one may be the difference in huge profits.

# Splitting up collections, lots & accessories

When you have purchased an item or lot that is packaged with accessories or if you have a collection of similar items you need to make a decision how to sell them. This is what separates the good sellers from the great and highly profitable sellers. A few examples of what I am talking about that I come across frequently:

- Digital / Film Camera with lenses, flashes, filters, case, etc

- PC with keyboard, mouse, monitor

- Home Theatre System (Remote Control, Manual, Receiver & Speakers)

- VCR with remote

- Complete series of a Comic Book run or Magazine

- Video Game Systems with games, remotes and accessories

- Complete box set of trading cards

- Broken electrics

I have only listed a few of the types of items that I have to make decisions about how I am going to sell them. There will be many times that you should make the decision to split up a packaged item, or a collection and sell pieces individually. The most simple thing to determine if possible is to research the value of each piece in a package or collection and do the simple math to see which will come out being worth more, and then you need to ask yourself if it is enough difference to make it worth your time to either combine items into a collection or to individually sell a packaged set of items.

This decision can be made for you already if the main item is defective in a package lot. If you have a complete home theatre system and the receiver is defective you can discard the receiver, or sell it as is if it has a good potential refurbished value. However if you have the whole system, you can sell the remote control, the user manual, and the speakers and maybe even make a profit when you would of taken a loss. The remote controls for stereos, receivers, vcrs, dvd players and especially older and harder to find units can have values in excess of $50, original user manuals can fetch an average of about $20 depending on the age, popularity of the item and how many other sellers are trying to sell the same thing. The speakers can also fetch you a nice sum of cash, this type of scenario has happen to me at least ten times with splitting up home theatre systems.

The receiver does not have to be broken for you to consider such a thing, when you are trying to sell a packaged set sometimes combined it can weigh a great deal and the shipping cost alone will cut deep into your profits. I had two of the same brand new home theatre system in the original packages and each one weighed 80 pounds and was shipped in two packages each. I sold one home theatre set as a complete package for $125 and the buyer had to pay $65 for shipping. I split up the other system and was able to make over $200 and a shipping profit of $20 so you can see how effective this can be, especially with heavier packages.

You need to make sure you do proper research which is the key to combining and splitting items. If you have the complete 1953 set of PlayBoy magazine your first thought might be to keep them together as a set, but you would most likely be losing a lot of money, view the following examples:

Here is a listing that described having a mint condition Monroe in it below:

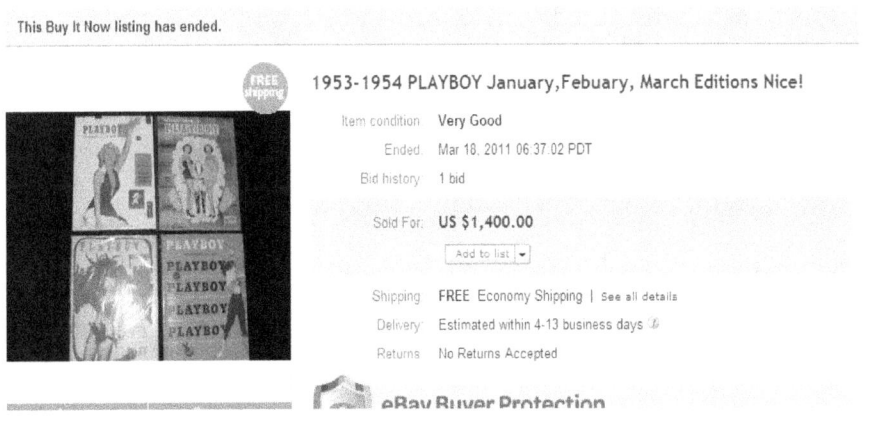

The first thing that you should notice is that the title in the second listing did not even have Marilyn Monroe in it. The single magazine should have been separated and focused directly on; the remaining pieces of the set can be sold individually or as a lot. Now obviously in the examples above the first one was an exceptional copy of the magazine but the point should be obvious owner took the time to have it graded and properly listed

You may also purchase to sell a lot of a particular type of item, and a few of those items are defective so what do you do? Say that you are an electronics buyer and seller and you have accumulated a quantity of defective video game systems that have virtually no value in non-working condition. Trashing the items may be the easiest thing for you to do, but putting together a lot of broken systems and selling them as a whole will provide you the ability to regain some of the losses that you would have taken by discarding them. After two years of collecting and selling cameras I had a box of twenty cameras that were broken that had good value if working and I sold them as a single lot for over two hundred dollars. I had another box of forty film cameras that were less than $10 resale individually and not worth my time selling them individually. I split the cameras up into two lots of twenty cameras and was able to make around $200 off of them.

# Pictures & Images

This could be the most important part of selling online and it is commonly rushed through and poorly done by most sellers that I see. You should invest in a nice camera, one that is capable of high quality zooming and at least 8 megapixels in my opinion. There are cell phones now that have cameras of this capability, for one I have a Motorola Droid Bionic that can take pictures of this quality. I don't recommend using your cell phone but if it is capable as a last resort it can do the trick. Make sure that you take a minimum of three pictures of every item unless you are absolutely certain that you can include every angle of an item or it is brand new in the original box, than a stock photo can do the trick. Here is an example of a bad picture:

Yes, this is actually a picture that I took a long time ago and used for a sale. There is part of my shirt in the left corner of the picture, there are books laying on the floor, a basket with trash in it, a box visible at the top and part of a guitar on the right. This is a horrible picture that shows pure laziness, can confuse potential buyers who might think other items are included, scare away buyers that think your laziness shows how much you care about the items you are selling or the value of them since you took no time to get it done. Don't do this! Here is an example of a nice photo:

As you can see in this picture there is no mistake about what is being sold, the item is clearly visible, there is no background and the pictures show only the item and accessory that it comes with. To create pictures like this you would need some editing abilities. It is not required to have pictures like this to sell them, as long as you have a solid background and no other items in the picture with decent lighting you will do just fine. Make sure you can get close up pictures as well, especially for used items as buyers are very wary about the condition of used items. If a seller takes a far away picture of a used item and includes nothing else most buyers will pass on the item or the seller will have to answer loads of e-mails of questions from buyers which will end up taking more of the sellers time then would have been required if time was taken to create better photos.

# The Psychology of Selling

The ability to sell an item to a buyer that you have never met or seen on the internet requires several things. Trust is in my opinion the most important part of successfully selling an item. The buyer must trust that you are accurately representing an item and that you will fulfill your end of the sales transaction by sending the item to them after they have paid for it. Trust can be built from feedback such as an eBay seller's rating, Amazon rating or any other marketplace's seller profile. In most cases buyers will be able to rate the transactions that they have had with the seller. This can be devastating to a seller if their performance has not been up to par.  Always make sure that a buyer receives exactly what you're selling and in the condition that you have stated, receives it earlier than the time frame required and that you have answered any questions that the buyer has asked before and after the sale in a timely manner. If there is a problem with the item and the buyer request a refund, return or any other request that you do whatever you can to assist the buyer if possible. This does not always mean that you provide them an instant refund if they request one or bend over backwards to make them happy. For instance I have had customers request refunds on products that they purchased six months before. This is unacceptable; my refund policy is 14 days for used items and 30 days for new items. I let the buyer know in the nicest possible way that I was sorry the product stopped working but policies are policies and mine was clearly stated so I was not going to provide a refund.

If you are selling on your own website or just want to provide the customer with complete assurance of trust you can use many different third party solutions. SquareTrade as an example is a company that you can sign up with and put a logo on your site or listing that guarantees customer satisfaction. They will help mediate any disputes and act as a middle man to ensure both the seller and buyer are satisfied with the transaction. They were one of the most reputable mediation companies for eBay until eBay decided they were not going to allow sellers to remove negative feedbacks. For many years you could pay a $20 fee and use SquareTrade to mediate a transaction with a buyer, if a positive solution was reached between the buyer and seller then a negative feedback left by the buyer could be removed. SquareTrade still is a viable option for E-Commerce sites and will provide a new seller with additional credibility. A few other sites to check out if you are interested in more creditability and building an image of trust for your customers are:

- Truste.com

- BBB.org

- Trustwave.com

- Bizrate Circle of Excellence

- VeriSign Secured Seal

- Web Safe Shield

- McAfee Secured Site

- Thawte

Another factor with online sales is to create a sense of urgency, this can be done with the use of auction sales, letting buyers know that the item won't last long and that you have the best price around. If you are simply selling products on your own random website with a picture and standard description and nothing exciting going on the customer may simply bookmark the item or move on somewhere else searching for the best price or better deal. If you show the quantities for example that you have in stock on the sales page this can also help in most cases.

Creating clearance and on sale items with prices slashed out for the MSRP and competitors prices is a long established and proven sales technique. I have a cousin that falls into this category of buyers; anytime there is a coupon or sale for something psychologically he thinks that he has to use it. For instance if he has a buy one get one coupon for say a Subway sub he will go out of his way to go get one before the coupon expires. It obviously is smart shopping to use coupons whenever you are going to buy something, but it is good to have them around for when you need to buy that item or food. My cousin is the type of buyer that will drive 20 miles to the nearest Subway to cash in his coupon thinking it is to good of a deal to pass up not realizing that he just spent his discounted sub savings on gas and time lost when there was plenty of food to eat at home or a closer food choice. A saying that I picked up from a friend of mine who is a business owner is "Never spend a dollar to chase a nickel". If you think about that phrase in terms of sales, we need to create demand, urgency and provide opportunity for buyers to spend a dollar for something that is only worth a nickel to us. If you're trading dollars for nickels you're going to do just fine in the sales business.

When you are putting an item up for sale and you drop the price and mark it as clearance or on sale make sure that you let the buyer know that this is a limited time offer. The sale will end at a specific time; this can create a lot of instant one click impulse buying. On the down side this can also create unsatisfied buyers and returns. Impulse buyers usually don't read product descriptions fully, ask questions about an item before purchasing it or really think deep about a purchase being right for them. When they get the item and it is not what they expected they can be quick to lash out, leave negative feedback and ask for refunds. Keep that in mind when you are selling, don't hide information in small fonts at the very bottom of your description as it can come back to haunt you. You can only burn people so many times before your reputation is worthless. Reputation is crucial for long term selling, anyone can door to door sell a new product for a few days but if that product is horrible the word will quickly spread and doors won't be opening for you any longer.

Make sure you clearly give the buyer a reason to buy the item from you and not somewhere else, tell them about your reputation and your customer satisfaction track record. Let them know that you will ship the next day or maybe offer free shipping or combined shipping for multiple purchases. For instance let it be known that if your customers spend over $100 then they will get free shipping, this will push a lot of customers who were only going to spend $80 or $90 to pick out another item that they were not going to necessarily purchase.

If you are selling a used item, antique, vintage or collectible item that is in fabulous condition then let the buyer know that your item is in one of the best conditions they will ever find. Point out flaws with other versions of your item that are being sold online and create a clear distinction in your buyers mind that your item is far superior to others.

## How to REALLY SELL on eBay

eBay has changed from what it once was, we can no longer list items for auction and sit back and watch multiple bidders fight over our items. The allure of online auctions has faded. The auction marketplace is flooded with millions of generic, poorly made and knock off goods mostly from China that make it hard for customers to find anything but nonsense. eBay was built around a community of collectors buying and selling quality used goods. eBay started offering sellers the ability to list 50 items free of charge for auction and monthly promotions to list unlimited quantities of items for auction which in turn has flooded eBay with garbage.

Sellers of used and collectible items are being pushed off eBay with strict new guidelines and requirements. Many sellers have left eBay completely to sell elsewhere. eBay has tried to bring in high volume sellers of new goods and forgotten about where they came from. The marketplace has rapidly changed but you can still make a fortune! It just takes a little more effort on your part. Don't get me wrong, there are still plenty of items that are perfect for online auction. Rare and unique collectibles still draw lots of bidders, antiques and vintage items do well too. The issue is with more common household goods, they are flooded throughout the market and it is hard to get top dollar for such items anymore.

So what is the best way to sell on eBay? Open a basic eBay store and sell 90% of your items in your store as a fixed price listing. Typically if I have items that are of value I will put them in my store at a slightly higher price than the marketplace research has shown it should sell for. I list the items with the GTC duration which is good till canceled, meaning the item will keep relisting every 30 days if it has not sold. I listed the items at a slightly higher price for two reasons; first if there is a buyer that absolutely has to have the item and is not concerned about price or saving a few dollars they will choose convenience over trying to bid online and get the item cheaper. Secondly, I list all items in my store with the "Accept Best Offers" feature. This feature will allow many potential buyers to place offers for your items, this will allow you to negotiate a better price for your item than selling it at auction and letting the chips fall where they may. If I have an item listed at $100 and a customer submits a best offer of $50 than the negotiating can begin. I can either accept the buyer's offer which will be a legally binding contract, just like if the buyer had won the item at auction or I can submit a counter offer, or even simply decline the offer. Generally I will counter with $90 in that situation to see how the buyer reacts. If the buyer was really submitting their best offer as $50 you will never hear from them again most likely and sometimes they will counter your offer with something like $55. Buyers can only submit three offers for an item so if I counter again the buyer will only be able to counter one more time before negotiations will end. If the buyer had submitted $55 than we are very far apart and I can tell we would have to meet around $65 or $70 in most cases here to make a deal. If the buyer had however come up to $70, we are getting really close and a counter offer of $80 will most likely seal the deal on this item.

That is the basic concept for successfully making great money on eBay as it stands in 2012. Maybe time will change eBay and the current economy flunk we have been in will fade and rejuvenate the markets, but until then you need to be safe and protect your profits and avoid losses! If you are selling with online auctions still then you will still want an online store with eBay to cross sell and promote items you have in your store. This is done by eBay displaying your other products available in your store on your online auction page listing. Make sure you make categories for your store and put items in the correct store categories so cross selling and promoting is done correctly. Here are a few tips that might help you out with selling on eBay:

- Download Turbo Lister

- Setup eBay Store – make categories

- Seller Manager Pro / Sales Reports

- Use TeraPeak to find the highest selling category for the product you are trying to sell, compare listing titles for the highest selling items and apply this to your listing.

- Use as many keywords in your title and description as possible.

- Use an HTML template for your listings to make your listing look professional and legitimate.

- Clearly state your policies and terms for the sale at the bottom of your listing description.

- Writing a clear, honest and accurate description of your item, eBay buyers are all about trust and honesty – don't get a mistrusting reputation or you'll be finished quickly.

- Offer free shipping on items that weigh a pound or less and worth at least $20.

- Extra features – add website logo or company logo if you have one.

- Add features like eTextAlert.com to your listing which allows buyers to send you a text message about your listing

- Adding a small streaming video of items that are used and of higher value; usually over $500 I do this so the buyer feels like he is standing in front of the item.

- Lastly make sure that you list items for auction at the most active time of the day and day of the week. This is usually between 5:00 PM and 6:30 PM on Sunday, then Saturday and Monday for the most part, use TeraPeak to view the best day and time for your specific product.

The eBay Seller Step-By-Step Checklist for Used Items:

1. Have I tested the item fully, is it fully functional? Would you guarantee it?

2. Is there any damage, dings, cracks, scratches or other problems that should be mentioned?

3. Can I ship this item out? How much does it weigh, what are the dimensions?

4. If I am shipping it will I have to buy any packaging materials? How much will it weigh packaged up? (larger packages can sometimes add 2 to even 10+ pounds, boxes alone can weigh several)

5. Will this item be oversized or irregular dimensions? Use UPS.COM/USPS.COM to calculate if large and irregular

## How to SELL on Amazon

If I want to sell a book or product on Amazon I need to first decide if it is new or used or collectible. The collectible category for items can only be listed by approved sellers on Amazon with a good track record of performance and feedback. The collectible category is for books that are for instance signed by the author, first printings, first editions, rare printings and other unique factors that distinguish the book from the rest of the crowd.

To determine the price of the book we are going to list we search for it on Amazon and see what the going rates are, sometimes you will see new books selling for $30 and the used price may be one cent. This is a very common occurrence as the market will usually be flooded with used books and kill the pricing power of them in some cases if the volume of a particular book sales are low and sellers are constantly bidding against one another without customers purchasing and keeping demand high.

If you are on the Amazon website and you type in the name of a product and click on the resulting product you will see on the right hand side of the listing a link that sells "Sell Your Copy" or "Sell on Amazon" which is what we can click to sell our product. Before you click on the sell yours link you will want to scroll down towards the bottom of the listing and find the rank number of the item under "Product Details". You can also type on your keyboard "CTRL-F" and then type "Rank" and it will jump you to the right spot on the page.

Product Details

Hardcover: 192 pages

Publisher: Sotheby Parke Bernet Pubns; illustrated edition edition (March 1988)

Language: English

ISBN-10: 0856673404

ISBN-13: 978-0856673405

Product Dimensions: 9.5 x 7.7 x 0.9 inches

Shipping Weight: 1.8 pounds

Average Customer Review: Be the first to review this item

Amazon Bestsellers Rank: #700,876 in Books (See Top 100 in Books)

Would you like to update product info, give feedback on images, or tell us about a lower price?

What we are looking to see here is the Amazon Bestsellers Rank, in this case for the item I was looking up it is 700,876. This number is definitely acceptable for us, anything under a million ranking is worth listing as it sells several times a year. If you see a ranking of say five or six million that may mean that only a copy or two have sold in the last year or even few years and that the market is very thin and you may have a long wait for it to sell. If you see that there is no ranking at all, this means that the book has never been sold before, at least not in the last several years and you may want to pass on listing the book. So moving on, were going to list this book and I click on the sell on Amazon button.

**Growing Up With the Impressionists: The Diary of Julie Manet**
**ASIN:** 0856673404
**Edition:** illustrated edition
**Binding:** Hardcover

---

Select the condition of your product

Please choose from the drop-down menu below after reviewing our condition guidelines. The listing of "Collectible" books about the approval process and Collectible Books Requirements.

Condition: New ▾

Add your comments about the condition

Please add a short comment to better describe the condition of your product. You are limited to 2000 characters.

Condition Note:
(Add your comments about the condition)
UNREAD BOOK - MINOR SHELF WEAR FROM AGE
Example: Dust cover missing. Some scratches on the front.

---

Now that I know the ranking is acceptable I will click the "Sell your Copy" link as previously mentioned. The book that I have chosen here is in new condition, it is over ten years old but it was never read. The thing to check on paperback books before considering them new is to look at their spine. When you look at the spine of a paperback book it will be creased if the book has been read and there will be signs of wear. If the book has any writing in it or stains, folded pages do not ever list this as a new book or you will run the possibility of being kicked off Amazon and having negative feedbacks making it very hard to sell. Just remember a book can still be considered new if it has been opened or flipped through. Take Barnes & Noble for example, customers walk in and read through books on the shelf and they put them back on the shelf when they are done. Do you think Barnes & Noble moves those books to a "Used Books Section" I think not.

Listing books under the used categories is virtually self explanatory; there are four possible choices of listing your used books. You can list them as Like New, Very Good, Good and acceptable. You can use your own judgment on the first three used categories because they are all similar shades of each other, however the acceptable category should become standard for the following: the book has moisture damage, there are a significant number of ripped pages, the binding is damaged or loose, there is writing or highlighting throughout the book and if there are pages missing from the book. All of these conditions must be listed in the item description section under Condition Note as seen in the previous image. If a book is missing the dust jacket but otherwise mint condition you can list it in the Used: Very Good category but don't try and get fancy and put it in the Like New category because a book that is like new will obviously include the dust jacket. Moving forward:

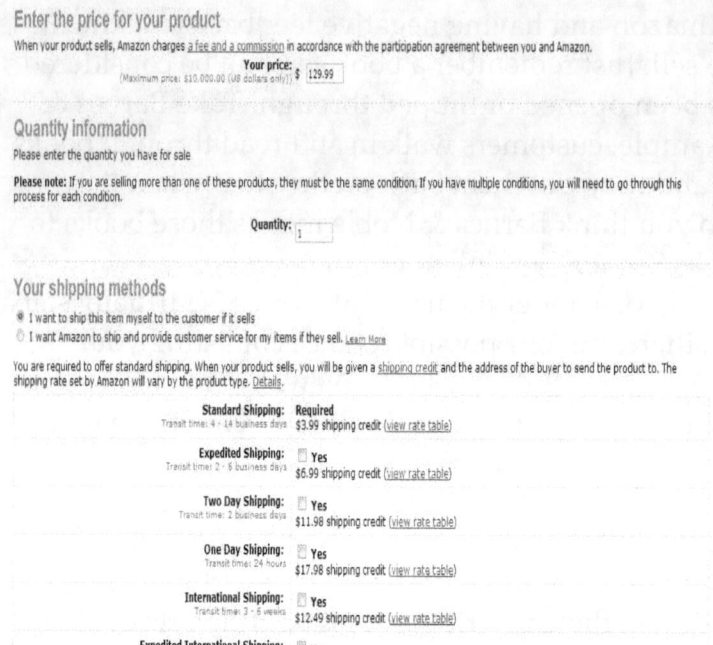

Enter the price for your product

When your product sells, Amazon charges a fee and a commission in accordance with the participation agreement between you and Amazon.

**Your price:**
(Maximum price: $10,000.00 (US dollars only)) $ 129.99

Quantity information

Please enter the quantity you have for sale

**Please note:** If you are selling more than one of these products, they must be the same condition. If you have multiple conditions, you will need to go through this process for each condition.

Quantity: 1

Your shipping methods

- I want to ship this item myself to the customer if it sells
- I want Amazon to ship and provide customer service for my items if they sell. Learn More

You are required to offer standard shipping. When your product sells, you will be given a shipping credit and the address of the buyer to send the product to. The shipping rate set by Amazon will vary by the product type. Details.

| | |
|---|---|
| **Standard Shipping:** Transit time: 4 - 14 business days | **Required** $3.99 shipping credit (view rate table) |
| **Expedited Shipping:** Transit time: 2 - 6 business days | ☐ Yes $6.99 shipping credit (view rate table) |
| **Two Day Shipping:** Transit time: 2 business days | ☐ Yes $11.98 shipping credit (view rate table) |
| **One Day Shipping:** Transit time: 24 hours | ☐ Yes $17.98 shipping credit (view rate table) |
| **International Shipping:** Transit time: 3 - 6 weeks | ☐ Yes $12.49 shipping credit (view rate table) |
| **Expedited International Shipping:** Transit time: 3 - 7 business days | ☐ Yes $35.98 shipping credit (view rate table) |

**Pricing Details for Your Product**

**Title**
Growing Up With the Impressionists: The Diary of Julie Manet

**List Price**
$39.95

**Competing Marketplace Offers**
11 All from $99.98
4 New from $129.99
7 Used from $99.98

**Amazon sales rank**
708,723

As seen in the first screen the new price for the book was $199.99, I went ahead and already listed this book which is why on the right side the new price reads $129.99. I have still pictured the next step in the process above as you would encounter in the listing process. You have several options for shipping but one of the drawbacks to listing on Amazon is that the shipping price is calculated by them. If a book weighs less than a pound you can feel comfortable clicking all of the available shipping options and not losing money in shipping. If you have a ten pound textbook and you have standard international shipping and one/two day shipping options selected you will be in serious trouble as you cannot send the book media mail when you offer expedited shipping services so keep that in mind when listing your books and shipping methods. The exception to the rule for me is if a book is of great value, $100 or more and the sales ranking is rather high for the book I will click all of the options and hope to expand my potential market to buyers from around the world and just eat the extra shipping cost. Shipping cost and inputting a price is the last step, just hit submit listing when you are done.

| | | | |
|---|---|---|---|
| **All** | New (4 from $129.99) | **Used** (7 from $99.98) | |

**Show** ⊙ New   FREE Super Saver Shipping offers only (0)

New 1-4 of 4 offers

| Price + Shipping | Condition | Seller Information |
|---|---|---|
| **$129.99**<br>+ $3.99 shipping | **New** | Seller: **bytecash**<br>Seller Rating: ★★★★ 98% positive over the past 12 months.<br>In Stock. Ships from MD, United States. Expedited shipping availab<br>International & domestic shipping rates and return policy.<br>UNREAD BOOK - MINOR SHELF WEAR FROM AGE |
| **$225.00**<br>+ $3.99 shipping | **New** | Seller: **Cambridge Bookstore Com**<br>Seller Rating: ★★★★★ 99% positive over the past 12 months.<br>In Stock. Ships from MA, United States. Expedited shipping availab<br>International & domestic shipping rates and return policy.<br>[Brand NEW ~ Hardcover with beautiful Dust Jacket , We Ship in 2<br>returns and work hard to ... ʺ Read more |
| **$285.00**<br>+ $3.99 shipping | **New** | Seller: **SCALES BOOKS**<br>Seller Rating: ★★★★★ 95% positive over the past 12 months.<br>In Stock. Ships from IN, United States.<br>Domestic shipping rates and return policy.<br>new |
| **$489.65**<br>+ $3.99 shipping | **New** | Seller: **AB_Art_Books**<br>Seller Rating: ★★★★★ 100% positive over the past 12 months<br>In Stock. Ships from NY, United States.<br>International & domestic shipping rates and return policy.<br>Flawless copy, brand new, pristine, never opened -- 200 pages.; S<br>Hardcover; New; |

This is my listing that we just created; as you can see the book is priced vary sporadically as new. I am hoping for a quick sale as this is not a book that sells everyday or even every week. If I wanted to hold out for six months I could most likely get the next highest price of $225 but in that same amount of time that I was waiting for the item to sell I could have done more with the money than the wait was worth.

What I mean by that last statement as I am sure some people are scratching their heads was that if I can sell it for $130 in a month or less than I would be able to reinvest my $130 in more inventory and turn it into at least $300 in a month and by six months time that money would have been turned over to have earned me around $5000. I did not pull that number out of a hat, and I am sure many people are still confused. With books on average I make over a thousand percent return but the flip rate is drastically slower, with instruments, electronics, clocks and cameras it is about a three to one return on average. Take the $100 for the book net profit which is a bit low even after fees and shipping and I can turn that into $300 net by the end of the month. The next month investing that $300 I would be able to spread it around a lot more and turn it into at least $1000 with inventory left over so in month three I will have turned that $1000 into a minimum of $2500 and in month four, five and six previous we will have a lot of carry over inventory that was not sold yet from the earlier months to include in our total sales. These carry over items will start pumping out our sales and should have accumulated into a significant flow of free money as our initial investments have already been covered.

You can fill in the rest of the picture and I can finish making my point which was that if I tried to hold out for a higher price and it took six months to get it than I would be $230 richer, if I take the quick money and keep taking the quick money and reinvesting it I would be looking at over $5k. This was merely meant as an example, I understand a lot more work would be involved to flip your money that many times and you would not have to lift a finger to collect the $230 (other than sliding a book into a padded envelope and printing a label). It really depends on your needs, you should not be holding onto inventory trying to sell it for the highest price if you are just getting started or are on a tight budget. The people who have huge bank accounts or people who are simply selling for a little extra money or a hobby and don't have time to put into flipping inventory are the ones who should be buying and holding. Personally now that selling is not my primary source of income I try to keep less than $20k worth of inventory at any particular time. This allows me to slowly but consistently make money at a pace that does not overwhelm the rest of my life.

Selling on Amazon is very simple as I just showed you,

there are however a few more little bits of information that you will need to understand in order for you to become an effective seller. Let's look at a few steps that you need to take after you have completed your listings. Look at the image below:

| Actions | Merchant SKU | ASIN/ISBN | Product Name | Date Created | Quantity | Condition | Your Price | Low Price | Status | Fulfilled By |
|---|---|---|---|---|---|---|---|---|---|---|
| Actions ▼ | 9N-DJK-U0SG | B00HG2SG4 | THE ROBERT AND JANE MEYERHOFF COLLECTION 1945 to 1995 [Paperback] | 06/28/2010 20:49:32 | 1 | New | $ 199.99 | ☁ | Open | Merchant |
| Actions ▼ | 4J-4176-IN4G | B00005B5YX | Hewlett Packard Laserjet 1220 Print/Copy/Scan Laser Printer [Electronics] | 04/02/2011 21:26:33 | 1 | Used - Very Good | $ 149.99 | ☁ | Open | Merchant |
| Actions ▼ | RK-6INX-YXK2 | 0856673404 | Growing Up With the Impressionists: The Diary of Julie Manet [Illustrated] | 07/06/2010 15:49:43 | 1 | New | $ 129.99 | $ 99.99 | Open | Merchant |
| Actions ▼ | 3K-KK2A-2O1N | B000I5N5YK | Canon PIXMA mini260 Photo Inkjet Printer (1444B002) [Electronics] | 07/19/2011 22:21:58 | 1 | New | $ 69.99 | ☁ | Open | Merchant |
| Actions ▼ | 2Y-TH7I-SZ8I | B004URPGAI | JVC RX-552V Audio Video Control Receiver [Electronics] | 06/19/2011 15:02:34 | 1 | Used - Very Good | $ 69.99 | ☁ | Open | Merchant |
| Actions ▼ | XH-KXJ7-NUMH | B00008VFK8 | JVC HRJ692U 4-Head Hi-Fi VCR , Black [Electronics] | 05/26/2011 23:25:24 | 1 | Used - Very Good | $ 59.99 | ☁ | Open | Merchant |
| Actions ▼ | XL-CS28-7HNZ | B001RW4YWA | Administration of the Navy Department in World War II [Hardcover] | 06/23/2011 19:31:10 | 1 | Used - Very Good | $ 58.99 | ☁ | Open | Merchant |
| Actions ▼ | U8-EV3Y-OH6L | B00085YP1M | The Cyclopedic Law Dictionary: With an Exhaustive Collection of Legal Maxims | 09/28/2010 18:21:57 | 1 | Used - Good | $ 55.99 | ☁ | Open | Merchant |
| Actions ▼ | QA-FNZM-W2U7 | 0394471318 | Autopsy of revolution by Ellul, Jacques | 09/06/2010 13:42:26 | 1 | New | $ 49.99 | $ 4.00 | Open | Merchant |
| Actions ▼ | PM-6XH6-311C | B00009ZW8J | MS1-PRO 5M522 1/4-Inch Angle Die Grinder [Tools & Home Improvement] | 04/01/2011 19:53:50 | 1 | New | $ 49.99 | ☁ | Open | Merchant |
| Actions ▼ | P4-9YV9-COTT | B002DGI1UK | Narration : four lectures / by Gertrude Stein; with an introduction by Thornt... | 06/28/2010 17:36:27 | 1 | New | $ 49.99 | $ 32.00 | Open | Merchant |
| Actions ▼ | MK-HHGV-6UHO | B001JZ4HC2 | The Perpetual Orgy: Flaubert & Madame Bovary [Hardcover] by Llosa, Mario Vargas | 06/28/2010 15:10:16 | 1 | New | $ 49.99 | ☁ | Open | Merchant |

This is a snapshot of a few items that are in my inventory on Amazon, you can find this area by logging into your Amazon seller account, and then clicking on view my current inventory under the Manage my Inventory section in the middle of the page of your seller account. As you can see there are two prices listed in the image, the first is my price and the next price is the low price on the marketplace for my product. The low price displayed is for the product that is listed in any of Amazon's categories. This is a huge change to their inventory system and a dreadful one for amateur sellers. Previously it would correspond with the same category meaning that if you have a new item listed for $19.99 and somebody else lists another new item of the same product for $18.99 and than someone else lists the item as used for $1.00 the low price would still reflect $18.99. This was a massive time saver because sellers would simply lower their prices by a few cents and you could decide if you want to lower your own price for the same item. Now with this new system in place you have to actually check to see what condition the low priced item is in. If your item is the low price for $99.99 as a new item but you see under manage your inventory the low price is $1.00 you have to check and see now if that person is listing a new book for $1.00 and completely killing your price or is it somebody listing a torn up acceptable book and they just want to get rid of it. For that very reason I do not recommend having more than a thousand items listed at a time unless you are going to use a 3rd party E-Commerce solution or software package to manage your inventory which I will discuss shortly.

I have about a thousand items so managing the items and constantly updating prices can be very tedious and time consuming. You will want to keep your inventory counts as low as possible with as many items as you can find that have a low sales ranking. If you just keep listing items that may never sell or you overprice everything or forget to change your bid prices you will accumulate a massive mess to go through. I know firsthand, about five years ago when I was in a bit of a financial pinch I did not want to throw anything away or lower and update prices for my items and after a year of doing so I had racked up over 3,000 items listed on Amazon. When an item would sell I had to be able to locate it in a short amount of time and also remove the listing from eBay and my personal website and anywhere else I also had it listed. This was a very chaotic way to run my Amazon business and over time I lost track of a few items and had to cancel orders and waste more time looking for the sold products than it took me to buy them and package them combined. Don't get me wrong, if books are your main source of income or you have sufficient space for massive bookshelves and an inventory tracking system in place or an alphabetical system for locating items by all means list your heart out. For the average seller like I was storing 3,000 books in my house was no picnic. My current system which supports 1,000 books is setup now with five book shelves, I have separated the paperback books, hardback books and leather bound books alphabetically by author. When a book sells I can grab it off one of the shelves in a matter of seconds. When the bid price for a book drops below $4.99 that is listed in the same condition as mine is I remove it from my inventory and recycle the book or put it in a pile for Goodwill to come by and pickup. That is a general rule of thumb, obviously if 10 sellers have the book listed at $100 and someone comes along and drops the price to $4 I am not going to get rid of the book or even lower my price. The simple strategy is to just wait it out and check back, usually when this happens sellers will start coming down on their prices and a new pricing point may be established for a book but it is all about supply and demand as you can imagine.

A very important factor you will need to keep in mind when you are selling on Amazon is your seller performance metrics.

### Performance Targets

All Amazon merchants should be working toward achieving and maintaining a level of customer service that meets the following performance targets. Failure to meet these targets does not necessarily put your account in negative standing, but failure to improve may negatively affect your account.

- Order defect rate: < 1%
- Pre-fulfillment cancel rate: < 2.5%
- Late shipment rate: < 5%

These are baseline goals. Merchants with exemplary performance have the opportunity to distinguish themselves to buyers through the feedback rating that appears next to each of their listings. Most merchants are exceeding these targets, so the stronger your performance, the better your chance of building a stronger, more competitive business.

---

The targets in the images above are the most important and you had better make sure that you are not falling behind. If you cancel an order for any reason, say you lost the item or broke it or sold it elsewhere but you let a sale happen on Amazon that goes against your order defect. The order defect rate is defined as the number of orders with a defect divided by the number of orders in the time period of interest. It is represented as a percentage. The target is less than 1% of your orders, I went on vacation last year and forgot to set my Amazon account status to vacation which temporarily suspends all your listings so customers can't complete purchases, as soon as you return you can set your status to back and all of your listings will come back online. I had 20 orders in the five days I was gone and I knew that I would not be able to ship them out by the time I got home in a timely fashion so I canceled all of the orders and Amazon responded by suspending my account for several months, I had to write a letter and convince them it was an accident and eventually I was reinstated. There is a new metric as of 8/1/2011 that requires all shipments to have tracking information which means you have to pay extra for delivery confirmation or ship with UPS tracking. This is not a big cost but if you are shipping out hundreds of very low profit margin items it will certainly cut into your profits. Currently after a customer purchases an item you will have two business days to ship out the item or you will be penalized on your metrics so keep that in mind if you are planning on being away for longer than a few days. Here is how Amazon vacation settings work taken from their website:

**Listings Status (Vacation)**

If you are going on vacation, or if you would like to temporarily remove your open listings for your self-fulfilled items from the Amazon website for any other reason, you can take advantage of our Listings Status feature. Just set your listings to inactive until you are ready to fulfill orders again. You no longer have to set inventory quantities to zero or extend shipping lead times, and can instead focus on your other pre-vacation tasks.

When you use the Listings Status feature, you won't have to set inventory quantities to zero or extend your shipping lead times. The Listings Status feature also provides a better experience for buyers by preventing them from placing orders that can't be fulfilled right away.

**Please note:** Before changing the status of your listings, you may wish to check for any pending orders, since these will not be automatically cancelled.

## Fulfilment by Amazon

When you set your Listings Status to inactive, only your open listings for your self-fulfilled items will be removed from the Amazon website. All listings fulfilled by Amazon through FBA will remain active.

## Changing Your Listings Status

To view your listings status in Seller Central, click the **Settings** tab and then **Account Info**. Scroll to the **Listings Status** section to see your current status.

To set your listings to inactive, click the "Edit" button, select "Inactive" and then click "Submit". Within 1 hour your listings will be unavailable for sale on Amazon's website.

When you are ready to sell again, simply go back to the Listings Status editing page, select "Active" and then click "Submit". Within 1 hour your listings will again be available for sale on Amazon's website.

**Please note:**
• Listings Status can only be edited by users who have been granted the right to manage inventory. If you do not see the "Edit" button next to Listings Status, you do not have authorization to change the setting.
• When your listings status is "Inactive," you will still be able to create and edit listings. Any additions and changes will be reflected on the website when you reactivate your listings.
• Any applicable monthly subscription fees will still be charged if it comes due while your listings are inactivated.

In order to list a product on Amazon it must be the exact product that is displayed in the catalog. What I mean by this is that if you are listing a VCR on Amazon and the product listing on the site says that it includes the remote control and you try and sell yours without one, even if you state in the description notes that yours does not have a remote control with it you may still be held liable. You had better find the remote control online at another store and purchase it from them or my personal favorite is to basically have the remote control drop shipped to my customer. I will send the VCR directly to the customer and place an order with the third party that is selling the remote and have them ship it directly to the customer. I like to do this because it saves me the trouble of having to buy a bunch of remote controls for different products that all might not sell. Make sure if you use this technique for any of your items that the seller your buying the accessory from has a guarantee for the product. If you are listing printers, iPods, cell phones and other electronics think twice to check the product listing for what is included before you list yours on the site. For instance some of those products may need the product instruction manual; some may need cables or installation cds. Recently I sold a Bogen answering machine to an international buyer which was brand new in the box, however someone had taken out the product manual that was with the unit and being lazy I did not check and the customer filed a claim with Amazon and got to keep the $199 answering machine and I did not get any of my money back. The same kind principal of the remote and manual should be followed throughout your listings, also when you are listing books be very careful about listing a book that has an Amazon listing publish date for example July, 1959 and your book is from 1958. I don't recommend that you list the 1958 in this category even if you put that in the description notes, however if your book was published March, 1959 by the same publisher than I would go ahead and list it there if there is not a more exact listing page found on Amazon and just write in the description notes that yours was published in March. When you are listing older books it will be a lot more common that you cannot find the exact year or edition that is listed in the Amazon catalog and you may have to list it in a year closest to the one you have, I did say that I don't recommend it but I will do it occasionally if the book has a great potential value. I have not had any negative feedbacks doing this and I have sold about 200 books like that. One final thing with listings that should go without writing but I will state it anyway, do not list a paperback book in the hard cover section and write in the description that it is a paperback because people will make purchases without reading your description notes which is my biggest concern with listing on Amazon. Don't list items that are AS IS and untested Amazon is not the place for that eBay is!

If you are planning on selling a lot of items on Amazon you may want to consider upgrading your standard individual basic seller account to an upgraded pro merchant. If you would like to create your own products that are not yet in Amazon's database catalog you can do so and upload pictures of the item(s) if you have an upgraded account. Also if you sell more than 40 items a month than you will be losing money in fees basically if you are not an Amazon PRO Merchant, below is how Amazon describes the plan.

## Upgrading Your Selling Plan

As your sales or inventory increase, you may question whether you should upgrade your selling plan to become a Pro Merchant.

1. Go to your Seller Account.

2. Under the Setting heading, click the "Seller Account" Information link.

3. In the Selling Plan section, click the "Upgrade" button.

4. Review the terms on the next page.

5. Click the "Proceed to Upgrade" button.

After clicking the "Proceed to Upgrade" button, you will be returned to your "Seller Account Information" page and see a message indicating that the upgrade process has begun. Your subscription to the new selling plan will begin immediately, and additional links to Pro Merchant seller tools will appear on your Seller Account page. Some billing features may take up to 30 minutes to become effective. Once the upgrade process is completed you will no longer be charged the $0.99 closing fee on your orders.


**Downgrading Your Selling Plan**

It's easy to test our Pro Merchant selling plan. If it's not the right plan for you, or if you no longer need access to features such as Create a Product Detail Page, you can downgrade your account and go back on the Individual selling plan.

To downgrade to an Individual selling plan, follow these steps:

1. Go to your **Seller Account**.

2. Under the Setting heading, click the "Seller Account" Information link.

3. In the Selling Plan section, click the "Downgrade" button.

4. Review the terms on the next page.

5. Click the "Confirm Downgrade" button.

When you downgrade your selling plan, your listings will remain active and available to buyers. Because your Pro Merchant subscription is billed at the beginning of each monthly cycle, your account and listings won't be downgraded immediately. Once your Pro Merchant subscription cycle ends, a $0.99 fixed closing fee will be assessed on each order.

If you are interested in selling on Amazon but don't want to worry about keeping track of your inventory and updating prices constantly or selling products on multiple marketplaces than you should consider a third party solution. The best solutions that I have used are Vendio.com and Andale.com. Vendio just bought out Andale so they are definitely still a growing force in the E-Commerce world.

- Vendio/3$^{rd}$ party inventory management,

  Webstore.Amazon, Make-a-store.com, Volusion.com,

  Shopify.com

- (selling items that match DESCRIPTION – buy

  remotes, etc)

It is also worth mentioning as a final note on how to sell on Amazon that after you create a seller account Amazon creates a mini store for you to promote your items like a website. It will automatically be created here http://www.Amazon/shops/<input your username here>

Amazon applies top secret and apparently very complex and technical formulas for their product rankings. The ranking figures that they display for products are in relation to how frequently a product sells on their site. Sales are measured hourly, daily, monthly and even yearly. It has been speculated that rankings are even determined by the amount of time between sales. There are more books than anything sold on Amazon and therefore books in the top 5,000 keep their rankings very consistently. Amazon does some "averaging" of sales to keep books from jumping up to number one just because you got all your family members in New York to buy a copy at exactly 2:00 PM on Sunday but it would be fun to watch for at least 30 minutes the book would have a terrific ranking!

Changes to Amazon sales rank is a great measure of the success of marketing efforts and hopefully a nice bump upwards in rank corresponds to a book promotion or event. Therefore if you are trying to sell a book in volume but you are afraid of the market dropping or what the true book ranking is there is something you can do to figure out a better understanding of the ranking. You can monitor the ranking of a book twice a week for about four weeks and then divide the result by eight. This has been suggested to be the true average ranking. Books that sit within the top 5,000 do not usually fluctuate by more than 20% and Amazon goes to great lengths to try and contain even that level of fluctuation. Titles in the

10-25,000 range may jump or drop by as much as 50 percent over a four month period. Books that are over 25,000 may swing rapidly.

**Amazon Sales Rankings - The General Consensus**

| Rank | Weekly Sales |
|------|--------------|
| 1,000 | 90 copies |
| 10,000 | 60 copies |
| 100,000 | 16 copies |
| 300,000 | 12 copies |
| 500,000 | 1 copy |
| 1,000,000 | 1 copy per month |

These numbers have been taken from the average of various online sources that claim to be able to calculate the value of the sales rankings. An accurate measure was taken from a publishing company that provided the sales results from their various books on the Amazon marketplace and compared those sales with the current rankings of the books on the marketplace.

If you have stuck with me thus far in this chapter I am going to leave you with a brand new strategy for quick selling on Amazon that maybe a few people in the world are utilizing. This will require you to have a phone with the Android market on it. I use the Motorola Bionic, and I have downloaded an app called HandyMarket and it is completely free! This app allows me to scan barcodes on any item and it will instantly pull up Amazon for me to sell the item immediately on the site with the product already found and the market value of the item along with sales ranking. It also will do a price search online for places to buy the product at lower costs. With this extremely valuable app I can go to any thrift store, pawn shop, auction house or even in some retail stores like Walmart and scan products to see what I can resell them for! I can have books, electronics, DVDs, etc listed on

Amazon before I even get through the checkout line. This app combined with TeraPeak on your phone or tablet will give you superiority over virtually every other reseller, especially at estate auctions where most of the buyers are older and rarely technologically savvy from my experiences.

# Chapter 6: Shipping & Handling

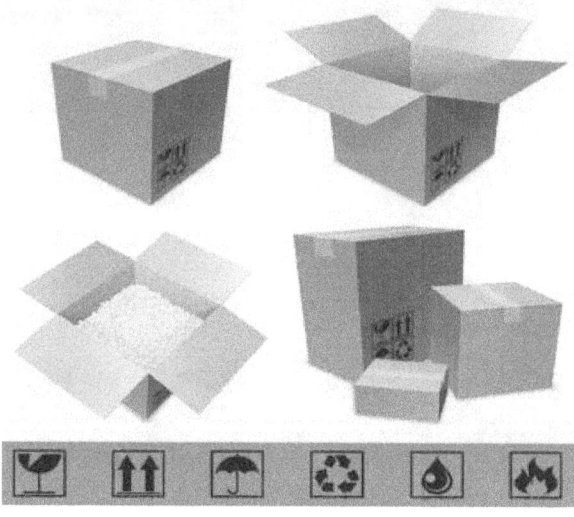

There may be a few secrets here that I can teach you so you can save yourself loads of time and money as well as keep your customers happy! First of all, before you sell an item or list it online you need to know what it will cost to ship out. You need to make sure you weigh the item in advance and measure it. Consider if you will need to buy any special materials in order to ship the item out. Special sized boxes can cost up to $20, crating and palleting an item can cost $50 or more. If it is a smaller item, say a printer that weighs 10 pounds and about average size then you need to quote the shipping to be at least 14 pounds when packaged to leave yourself some room for packaging and the weight of the box. The shipping box can be deceiving and add a lot of extra weight depending on it being corrugated and materials used. Some boxes can weigh as much as 50 pounds, a common box that is used in freight is called a gaylord, bulk bin, or corrugated pallet box and it is usually made of triple wall corrugated fiberboard. These are used for bulk packaging and were initially produced by Gaylord Container Company of Gaylord, Michigan. A gaylord box is often 48" x 40" x 36" (approx. 120 cm x 100 cm x 90 cm) and fits neatly on a standard shipping pallet. Yes, I know that was an over the top example but I want you to think twice about the packaged weight of an item. Another solution that would solve this dilemma would be to prepackage the item. This might cause two new problems for you however, if you prepackage your items and a customer buys multiple items from you they will expect a combined rate discount and you will have to unpack the item. Also you run the risk of a customer asking you a question about the item that would require you to open up the package and take it out to answer. There is also the chance that the item won't ever sell and it will just sit around taking up space.

Another thing that should be considered before we actually package anything up is the "handling fee". This can be whatever you want it to be, you can set this up on eBay in your Turbo Lister file or when you're doing your listing online. Consider a reasonable charge, I usually have four standard charges – the minimum is $2.50 and I use this for items that I can package up in less than ten minutes and don't require me to purchase a box or any special materials. If that seems high for an item that weighs 2 pounds, then think about the padded envelope I just stuck it in or the tape I used for the box and the toner that will be used to print the label and the fees that eBay charges me as final value fees on my shipping cost. It becomes virtually break even or a loss usually. The next fee I use is $5.00 which is for items that will take me more than 10 minutes to package up or possibly will require me finding a special box or even buying a smaller one. The third fee is $20 and I use this anytime I have to ship out an item weighing more than 50 pounds as they typically require a great deal of packaging materials and a double corrugated box at minimum.

Lastly is one I don't really use anymore but I used to use all the time and buyers never had a problem with it; $50 and that was for any item that required a pallet or wooden crate/box to ship it in. I used to sell a lot of extremely heavy restaurant equipment and it could take hours sometimes to get an item like that properly on a pallet and secured and usually the use of a fork lift or several people pulling their backs out to lift it up. Pallets are usually close to $50 to have them ordered but that is a fee I've never paid, you can find usually dozens of them laying behind any shopping center on the ground after trucks have dropped off their loads.

A few basic materials you will need to be able to handle most shipments:
- A tape gun!
- Double length tape (I usually get them at staples, about $15 for a six pack but I can ship out a hundred or more packages). Buy in bulk, individual roles are ridiculously overpriced!

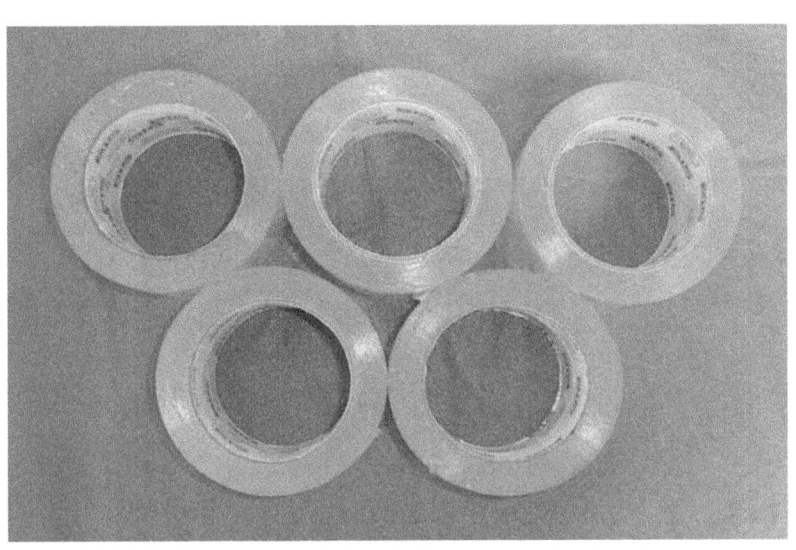

- Shrink Wrap/Stretch Wrap Film (I usually buy 4 packs of 80 gauge shrink wrap – 18" long tubes that are 1500

feet long) The average rate on eBay is around $45 for this.

- If you are shipping out books, or smaller items I suggest buying some padded envelopes – my standard order on eBay is for 100 9.5x14.5 KRAFT BUBBLE MAILERS PADDED ENVELOPES – you can use that term if you'd like – I get them shipped for about $25 – makes shipping books and small items a cinch!

- Access to cardboard boxes, if you are planning on doing a lot of shipping, you might want to go ahead and sign up for uline.com they are pretty much the best in the business for shipping products. If your going to take it as it comes than find yourself a local shopping center and get boxes from the dumpsters behind the stores, walk into the store and ask the manager for empty boxes. I get mine from Office Depot and Staples – I know the people there and they save boxes for me.
- Packaging materials – I also get my materials from the shopping center, they discard huge bags full of bubble wrap, shrink wrap, foam, peanuts, Styrofoam and other valuable shipping materials. The cost of each bag that I get free is worth about $50 at Staples so you can save a

ton! If you can't find anywhere to get them free you can always pay for packaging materials or use the always plentiful and easy to come by newspaper. However, customers do not like getting items shipped with newspaper as it can be very messy and you won't like the way your hands look after your done packaging either. If you must use newspaper than wrap the item you are shipping with the shrink wrap and then lay it in with newspaper under and all around it – that way the item won't get ink all over it. Just a few times around to cover it, as I have done below:

- You will need a scale; you don't need anything fancy like you would see at the UPS store that weighs your item and connects to your computer to print out a label. A good old fashion floor scale will do the trick for anything over 5 pounds usually, obviously heavier items can be a pain this way because you have to weigh yourself holding the package and then weigh yourself and hope nobody is looking over your shoulder when you do. If you are using a floor scale than you will have to also have a smaller scale that can do ounces, you can find these for fewer than ten bucks, a baby scale would work as well. Every ounce counts when the item is less than 13oz for first class USPS domestic so make sure you weigh it exact. For international shipments anything under 4 pounds first class international you need to get the weights exact. Remember when you're weighing an item and it weighs 10 pounds and 1 ounce than it weighs 11 pounds. You have to always round up or you will get hit with adjustments, usually not very often from USPS if it is close but UPS is very strict and over the years I've had at least a hundred adjustments done. The same applies when you are measuring your package, you have to round up. Be careful not to package something in to large of a box that it goes into another class such as oversized 2 and 3, a single inch could mean the difference between $20 or more. Shipping is a lot about size, you can have an item that weighs 5 pounds and it can cost you $50 to ship it if the box is to big. UPS using a dimensional weight system which uses multiple factors. Here is what I mean by that:

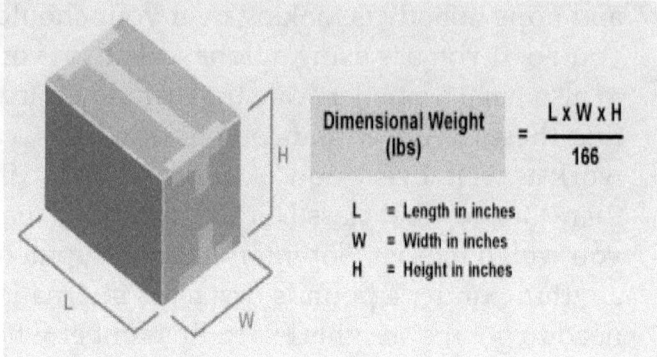

Dimensional Weight (lbs) = $\dfrac{L \times W \times H}{166}$

L = Length in inches
W = Width in inches
H = Height in inches

For domestic shipments:

<u>UPS Air Services shipments</u>: Divide the cubic size in inches by 166 to determine dimensional weight in pounds. Increase any fraction to the next whole pound.

<u>UPS Ground shipments:</u> If the cubic size of the package in inches is 5,184 or larger, divide the cubic size by 166 to determine dimensional weight in pounds. If the cubic size in inches is less than 5,184, use the actual weight of the package.

<u>How To Measure Your Package Size</u>

To measure ground packages use the following formula:
Length + 2x Width + 2x Height

Step 1. Determining Length

Measure the longest side of the package, rounding to the nearest inch. This is your length.

Step 2. Determining Girth (2x Width + 2x Height)

Measure the width of the package, rounding to the nearest inch. Multiply this number by 2.

Measure the height of the package, rounding to the nearest inch. Multiply this number by 2.

Add these two numbers together. This is your girth.

Step 3. Add the length and the girth together. This is your package measurement.

Step 4. Weigh the package to obtain its actual weight.

An important factor to consider when shipping is when to buy insurance. All UPS shipments are automatically insured up to $100 which is great, and trust me you'll need it sooner or later. When I first started selling online I was told by a buddy who had been doing it for a long time to make sure that I package every item as if it is being sent to hell and back. With UPS I have filed over 30 claims in the last ten years, but I have also shipped out close to 10,000 packages with UPS so the ratio is not all bad. There were times when I could have filed about 50 more claims but it was easier to just issue a small partial refund for the buyer. If the item damaged is worth less than $50 total than I don't file a claim, if you file to many claims guess what happens? Yeah you guessed it UPS quietly raises your rates just like an auto insurance company does with accidents and points. One benefit that I love with UPS is the free tracking information that is included with your shipment, that way your customers know exactly where the package is and when they can expect it to be delivered.

Shipping Domestic with USPS on the other hand does not include insurance so keep that in mind if you are shipping out a $90 piece of fine china and the rate for UPS is $10.90 and USPS is $9.90. Don't try and squeeze out that extra buck, do the math and ask yourself if you're willing to lose $90 when you could have covered it by paying the extra dollar with UPS, or paying the extra fee for USPS insurance which is more than UPS charges. Here is the insurance rate table for USPS:

# INSURANCE FEE RATES

| Fee | Insurance Coverage |
|---|---|
| $1.65 | $0.01 to $50 |
| $2.05 | $50.01 to $100 |
| $2.45 | $100.01 to $200 |
| $4.60 | $200.01 to $300 |
| $5.50 | $300.01 to $400 |
| $6.40 | $400.01 to $500 |
| $7.30 | $500.01 to $600 |

$7.30 plus $0.90 per $100 or fraction thereof over $600 to $5,000.

Make sure you protect yourself, your customers and your reputation by insuring items that are of a fragile nature which should be self explanatory. Also insure items that are valuable, as in valuable enough for you to not want to eat the cost of a refund if the item goes missing after you ship it out and again this should just be common sense.

I am asked about shipping registered mail a lot as many people don't understand when it should be done. There are only a few reasons that I ever ship using registered mail; one is when I have an item that is worth more than a $1000 and it is small enough to fit into an envelope or small box the size of a shoe box. Typically items of this nature would be valuable coins, trading cards or jewelry. Another rare occasion that I do it for is when an item is under 4 pounds and is being shipped internationally to an unstable country per say and the item is worth more than $500. When you ship out an item using registered mail the package is completely sealed at the post office in front of you, they use heated corrugated tape and seal off the box or envelope so that when your item arrives at its destination and it is still sealed there is no question or doubt that what was it in originally has not been removed along the way. The minimum cost for shipping registered mail starts at $10.75, even if it is an envelope your shipping that weighs less than an ounce. The reason that the cost is so high and USPS takes such great lengths to protect the package is because this type of mail can be insured for up to $25,000! Regular insurance through USPS can only be insured up to $5,000.

# Filing an insurance claim:

I am not going to link to the forms you need to go to on USPS, UPS or FedEx or any other shipping service for that matter because I don't want to have to edit this section every month when they change. Do a search on any of the sites for insurance claim and you will have no trouble getting where you need to be. If you want to file a claim with UPS it is a fairly long process. Pick up your phone and call 1-800-PICK-UPS, there is no option for filing a claim on the menu so you have to say it and hope the system recognizes the request. After about ten minutes of making your way through automated messaging systems you will finally get to an operator. All you need to do is provide them with the tracking number of the damaged or lost package. State the value of the claim you are making and you better be able to verify it. They will send you the paper work in the mail a few weeks later and you have to fill it out and prove the value of the item and the amount you are claiming. I usually print out a copy of the sales record on eBay or a comparable item if I am making a full claim, if I am making a partial claim than I show them the cost to repair the item and mail it back to them. Hopefully all goes to plan and they don't go and inspect the package at your customer's house. If they decide not to inspect the package which they almost always do for claims under $200 then you are home free and a check will be in the mail. It usually takes about 30 days from start to finish with most claims I have filed. Keep your customer informed of what is happening and if UPS says that they do not need to inspect the package or in some cases they will recover the package if the claim was of higher value, but if this is not happening you can refund your customer with the assurance your money is on the way. I have always received a check after that point, sometimes customers are willing to wait for you to get the check in the mail patiently, other times they will demand an immediate refund and if you don't provide them with one they will file a claim against you through eBay, PayPal or the credit card company if the transaction was not done through eBay. If UPS decides that they want to inspect your packaging and the damaged item, which they will do if you have been filing a lot of claims and you better cross your fingers that you packaged it according to specifications. For instance was the box rated for the weight of the item? If you put a 50 pound item in a box that was only rated for 30 than claim denied immediately. Did you leave at least 4 inches of space in all directions around the item that was in the box? Claim denied! Did you use a used box, had it been shipped with before or used in any other way before you shipped it out? If so…DENIED! And lastly did you use appropriate packaging materials, if you used plastic trash bags to secure a printer, well you get the point. I have had two claims denied in my experience and I had to eat the cost of the item plus shipping and provide the customer with a full refund. Make sure you don't cut corners with shipping.

USPS insurance is a lot similar to get through, you can do everything online by filing out a few forms, providing proof of value which can be done by pasting a web link to your product sold. Let them know the claim amount and you'll have your check in about two weeks. However, insurance is not available on services like USPS International First Class or Priority International flat rate so they try and make you pay ridiculous cost to upgrade to express or registered mail. I have filed only five USPS claims out of 30,000 packages shipped out, but out of those shipments only about 1000 were ever insured. If they had all been insured I would have filed about a 100 claims by now. Damage has not been my problem, sending packages internationally; especially with first class has been a nightmare. I have had about five claims from customers in the last year that they did not receive their items. They file a claim with eBay, guess what I did not insure it, denied! They get their money back and you get nothing. So your saying why don't you require priority mail shipping? Not many customers are willing to pay more than the item is worth in shipping which can be an easy $30-$40 for priority shipping for an item that weighs 4 pounds. They only alternative is to send it flat rate in an envelope which can be done for about $15. This is only an option when the item is not fragile as there is no room for packaging in a thin envelope. Long story short, I hardly sell anything internationally anymore unless it is over $100 and I require priority or express shipping service and the customer agrees. Here is the insurance timeline from the USPS website relating to how long you have to file a claim and how soon:

File claims as follows:

a.*Damaged or Missing Contents:* customers should file a claim immediately but must file no later than 60 days from the date of mailing.

b.*Lost Articles:* customers must file a claim within the time limits in the chart below.

| MAIL TYPE OR SERVICE | When to File (from Mailing Date) | |
| --- | --- | --- |
| | No Sooner Than | No Later Than |
| Express Mail | 7 days | 90 days |
| Express Mail COD | 45 days | 90 days |
| Registered Mail | 15 days | 180 days |
| Registered COD | 45 days | 180 days |
| Insured Mail | 21 days | 180 days |

| | | |
|---|---|---|
| COD | 45 days | 180 days |
| APO/FPO Insured Mail (First-Class Mail, SAM, or PAL) | 45 days | 1 year |
| APO/FPO Insured Mail (Surface Only) | 75 days | 1 year |

Shipping and handling smaller items are a usually piece of cake, however when you try and ship out items that are either very large or very heavy things get difficult. It is hard to accurately quote shipping prices on larger things that are not packaged up. Below are the restrictions for the maximum weights and dimensions of the main carriers.

## USPS

- Maximum weight: 70 pounds
- Maximum length + girth: 130 inches
- Costs almost triple for Parcel Post shipments that are "oversized" (Length + girth is greater than 108 but less than 130 inches)

## UPS

- Maximum weight: 150 pounds
- Maximum length: 108 inches
- Length + girth: 165 inches
- Oversize surcharge of $40 once length + girth exceeds 130 inches

- Fee if maximum limits are exceeded: $50 for over maximum weight; $50 for over maximum length; $50 for over maximum length + girth

## FedEx

- Maximum weight: 150 pounds
- Maximum length: 119 inches
- Maximum length + girth: 165 inches
- Oversize surcharge of $40 once length exceeds 108 inches or length + girth exceeds 130 inches

If you decide you want to ship an item using freight, consider a few things; if you are shipping from a residence there will be an extra $50 charge for the delivery truck to come pick up your item and there will be a $50 charge for having to use a lift gate. A lift gate is the device that picks up your pallet or container from the ground. If you were at a commercial loading facility they could back the truck right up to the doors and slide it on. UPS and FedEx both offer freight shipping, I suggest you check out www.freightcenter.com/ebay.aspx if you want to know more about freight shipping, they are eBay's certified freight shipping processor. There are two ways that I avoid paying these fees; if the customer wants the item I make them arrange the shipping, this means their invoice, their billing information, I just prepare the item on a pallet and sit it outside my house and the customer handles making the arrangements for picking it up and I pay nothing. The other way is to cut out the middle man, I use a company called Forward Air and another known as Old Dominion. They offer direct drop offs at their locations at the airport so the item does not have to be picked up here locally, however they just make sure it gets on the airplane and to the destination. In most cases your customer will have to arrange for a company to pick up the shipment at the airport and bring it to them. I do not have a truck for hauling so I rent a truck for $19.99 at The Home Depot, plus any gas and I can use it for four hours. I usually charge the customer $50 extra and let them know that up front for my time and cost involved.

## Free Shipping:

Lastly the idea of free shipping has rapidly blown up in online sales and is now very common for smaller items. eBay tried to close a loop hole that sellers were using to sell items for .99 cents and charge $20 for shipping an item that weighed a pound or two. Customers were not always happy about this but they still got a great price. eBay however got screwed as they only charged a final value fee based on the sale price so with customers selling products for pennies they were not making enough money. Now you be charged a final value fee based on the total which includes shipping, there are also final value fee discounts for sellers who offer free shipping and the DSR rating system that eBay has in place gives the seller an automatic 5 stars and a higher rating in the search results on eBay so there are benefits. It really comes down to profits, if you can sell an item for $50 that weighs under a pound you would be wise in offering free shipping as you can send the item priority mail for around $5 and the customer is happy they didn't pay for shipping and your happy because you will sell at a higher percentage rate. This is about all I am going to cover on shipping in this edition of the handbook, I could write another 500 pages on shipping alone!

# Chapter 7 - Individual Scenarios

It was proposed to me a few years ago that not everyone is capable or in a position to deploy my tactics and strategies to start generating income. I have also heard people's excuses for not improving their financial situations stating that it takes money to make money and that only rich and wealthy individuals can invest and start a business. I would like to first dismiss these statements and address the real problem at hand with these individuals' mindsets. They are close minded, cowards, without confidence in themselves or their abilities or just outright pessimist. I am reminded of a famous saying in a book known as *The Art of War* which states that every battle is won before it is even fault. If you think about that and apply that to making changes in your life or venturing into a new business you can see the reality behind this message. Basically stated, if you don't think you can accomplish something or you are expecting to fail it will become a self fulfilling prophecy and you will undoubtedly fail. Whenever I start something new or start a task at all I always think about what the great Yoda from George Lucas's Starwars series said "Do, or do not, there is no try!" So either start things with the mentality that you will succeed and finish what you start or don't start them at all and save your time and energy. One of the greatest fuels of self-doubt and a poor self-worth is quitting. If you make a habit of quitting and letting yourself off the hook when stricken with adversity it will become a habit and a reaction. Faced with pressure and stress your mind will naturally begin to make excuses for why you can't finish something and the inevitable exit strategy will be to give up. Not that you should live your life based on a fantasy characters mantra but the underlying message is clearly meaningful in this case.

When I was young I was told a story about elephants and how they are kept in captivity so easily. The story began with a man in Africa walking down the street and spots a massive elephant with a rope tied around his leg connected to a stake in the ground. The man is baffled by this image and locates the owner of the elephant for questioning. He locates the owner and trainer of the elephant and asks the man what is stopping the elephant from breaking free and running away. The trainer replies by first stating the obvious that the massive creature could easily snap the rope and flee. What he says next I feel holds true for many individuals and even at times in my own life. "The elephant, at a young age when it was much smaller was tied up with the same rope and to the same stake in the ground. The elephant fault hard and persistently tried to break free from the binds but was not strong enough to do so. As time passed the elephant lost the will to keep fighting for freedom and became conditioned to believing that it was not strong enough to break free from the rope so it stopped trying all together."

At a young age this story had little meaning and purpose to me. I was always very competitive and an extremely confident person and a bit of a rebel. There was nothing that I wanted to do that I believed I could not accomplish. When we are young we are more fearless and less adverse to risk taking because we have not tasted failure, we have not felt the pain of defeat. I shared with you earlier my story of failure running a business and eventually having everything taken from me. I went into a very dark place for several years after this failure and lost the belief that I could be successful in life as a businessman or an entrepreneur. The fear of failing again and the fear of feeling that pain and embarrassment of failure and disappointment took hold of my mind. Negative thoughts are like a cancer and they will spread and grow until eventually they take over your entire body. If you don't stop negative thoughts and separate yourself from negative individuals they will become you and your chance of treatment diminishes with each passing moment.

I was raised in a middle class family and surrounded by educated working class individuals and social groups which conditioned me into believing that I needed to go to college and get a job to fall in line with normal way of life. The difference between upper class families and the conditioning which is common amongst middle and lower class upbringings is that the rich and wealthy normally don't put chains on life's potential for their offspring. Many of the wealthy families condition their children to become leaders of men, innovators and creators. If you have gone through life believing that education or a good job is the only real chance you have for living a good life than maybe you need to open your eyes and break the chains that have held you back from becoming what you truly desire. Your first attempts at a different path from the normal one may fail, but never fail to make an attempt.

Having a good job may be enough for you to truly lead a happy and fulfilling life and that is great and I fully support those who take that route. However those who have a dream to do something different but never take their shot at pursuing it I feel sadness for them. I have known many folks who hold their deepest regrets in never taking a chance at living their dreams. They went to school and got a job and told themselves it was only temporary and they would eventually go after what they really wanted. Time passed by, they got a promotion or two and took on a mortgage, had children and believed they did not have time, money or the will to make changes in their lives. One day they wake up and realize that they hate their lives, hate their jobs and are stressed to the limit. Even at this point it is never too late to fight for what's important to you, never too late to go back to school; never too late to start a business and it is never too late to pursue a dream.

Maybe none of this chapter applies to you thus far, you may still be in high school or college or maybe your even homeless you can still start earning extra income and financial freedom regardless of your current position in life. A lot of this book is based around psychology and thought processes for a reason. I can lay out exactly the steps for someone to take and exactly what needs to be done to reach a goal or make a certain amount of money but it is all pointless if your mindset is such that you can't do something. I feel that if I can change even a few individuals mindsets and open their eyes to possibilities than that will take them further then conditioning them to follow a process or a list of tasks. Only when you can see the world as an endless expansion of possibilities and opportunities will you be able to accomplish anything.

To continue the open minded thought juices and to touch upon some of the situations and scenarios I have been confronted with in the past for not being able to become financially independent I have come up with a few situations which may be relevant to your current one. Please keep in mind that I am not an attorney or legal advisor and that these are only actions that I would take if I were in the following situations. The methods that are discussed are based on those found within the scope of this book.

# You are Homeless:

You may be one of the many homeless people that I have given this book to on the side of the road as you were begging for money or food. If this is the case then you are already ahead, after you have read this book you can resell it as an added bonus. Therefore I have given you free knowledge and money.

Overcoming your financial situation and taking back your life may be one of the hardest things to do. If you cannot find a job, unable to work or otherwise refusing to look for a job than I propose the following means of action that may help lift you from your financial troubles. Don't think me naive, I realize that there are homeless people out there that are alcoholics, drug addicts and downright lazy individuals. If that is the case than I cannot help them until they are willing to help themselves. However, if you are willing to beg others for money then you should have no shame in doing some of the following income producing strategies.

I will assume the role as the homeless person now to make it clear that I am not telling you what to do as some of the following may fall into a bit of a gray area but nothing illegal.

I have no money, not a penny to my name, no credit cards, no bank account, no car or family and friends to turn to for money or support. I have the clothes that are on my back and a backpack with my few possessions which include this book which I am going to use as a survival guide. I sleep at the local homeless shelter and I eat at the local soup kitchen. My basic needs are taken care of as in every major city in the United States there are shelters and soup kitchens so I don't need money for survival; however there are nights when the shelter is full and I have to sleep outside. There are also days when I don't make it to the soup kitchen on time or they run out of food.

I am not a criminal and I don't want to steal to have to survive. I need to figure out a way to make money without any starting capital or assets of any value. I need to find a computer with internet access in order to use the knowledge I have learned in this book or an address book so I can locate places of interest. I walk to the closest library in my town which has free public internet access. I locate the following locations within walking distance and write down or print out the addresses, phone numbers and directions:

- Several close by shopping centre and outlet malls
- A list of pawn shops
- A list of consignment and second hand stores
- A list of estate auction and consignment auction companies
- A list of book exchanges
- Local dump or scrap station
- Local movie theatres

I exit the library and head to a local shopping outlet with many other local stores on the main road. I go behind the facilities and locate their dumpsters. I know that most stores will throw away packaging materials and broken merchandise and sometimes they will discard old stock that they couldn't sell. For the next several days I sift through the dumpsters behind the local book super store, the local stationary store and video rental store. I gather up several shopping carts full of bubble wrap, cardboard boxes, scrap metal, boxes of discarded books that the book store could not sell of which most of them are holder editions of books and clearance books and I also gather several bags of empty DVD cases, movie posters and other movie collectibles that were discarded by the video store when promotional new releases are over. I find some nice secluded place to hide all of my findings, maybe in the woods or an abandoned or condemned house somewhere they will be safe.

Next on my journey I travel to the two local movie theatres in my area and what do you know I find several massive discarded movie standees from the latest movie to leave the theatres. I take them back to my secret stash and head to the local book exchange. The book exchange allows me to take as many free books as I want without paying or having to actually exchange any books. I grab all the law books, medical books, investing books and textbooks that I can fit in my shopping cart and fancy my way out of there. I know the books are stamped with "This is a free book not for resale" but I'm homeless I think they will understand as they are a non-profit company who donates books to those in need.

I make another stop at the local library and create a free e-mail account. I use this e-mail account to make a Craigslist account which won't require me to have a credit card and several other free classified posting sites. I post an ad selling a lot of packaging and shipping supplies, another ad selling 300 of the 500 books that I have accumulated of lesser quality and potential value from the local book store dumpster and book exchange. While still at the library I write down a list of swap meets and local exchanges.

I leave the library to go sleep at the homeless shelter and borrow the phone there or borrow one from one of the staff members and I call the local estate and consignment auction companies for available tables or rows, maybe one at a local fairgrounds or one within walking distance of my well hidden stash of merchandise. I find one that will accept my collectibles and shipping supplies. I know that buyers at a consignment or estate auction are typically resellers and dealers so they will need bubble wrap for sure so I roll it up and put it in plastic bags that I found in the dumpster making it presentable. I take the movie standees and merchandise along with the DVD cases to the auction, I also throw in the 200 remaining books that I got from the exchange and the dumpster and I mix them together and make sure to include the new books from the book store in each lot. I split the 200 books into ten separate lots each with new and used books in it.

The next day I track on down to the library and see a lowball offer for my 300 books of $100, I have no money so I have to take what I can. I see another offer for packaging supplies of $50 and I have to take that as well, I know I could do better if I waited because a small roll of bubble wrap sells for $10 and I have bags upon bags of it but I need money so I accept both offers and have the buyers meet me at a respectable location and only accept cash.

The next day I go back to the auction where I dumped my items off to see how they do and collect my money. I talk to everyone I can that is doing a lot of bidding at the auction, I collect business cards, phone numbers and get details on what they buy and sell for future reference. I ask bidders that I have been talking to who have been buying huge lots if they want everything in the table lot or row lot that they won and many of them let me take some items that they don't want. At the end of the auction my five garbage sized bags of bubble wrap sell for $50, my movie standees brought in only $50, the bags of empty DVD cases a modest $20 and my 10 individual box lots of books sold for $10 each giving me $100 total from the books and $220 total from the auction. I net $180 after the auction house takes their fees so now combined with my $150 from Craigslist sales I am sitting with $330 and feeling better about my situation, I go buy a happy meal instead of eating at the soup kitchen to spoil myself for once.

I take all the scrap metal that I had been collecting from the dumpsters and haul it in shopping carts to the scrap station or dump and add another $30 to my bankroll. I wait for the next estate auction or consignment auction nearby and I go armed with my $300. I purchase a few instruments, antique clocks and cameras and other items that a pawn store or antique/consignment shop would take and a few things I can pop real quick on Craigslist. I need money fast so I have to basically sell at wholesale to the pawn shop and antique store but I still double my money and now I have over $600 and I have made it.

I wake up early the next day and purchase a pre-paid credit card, one that does not require me to have a credit history or bank account but allows me to do something amazing, setup an eBay account, Amazon account, PayPal account and other accounts where I can sell merchandise. I use the soup kitchen or homeless shelter as my address for the credit card and on my seller address information. I am not able to sell and accept payments everywhere yet until I have my bank information. I go to yard sales now, thrift stores, estate sales, and business liquidation auctions. I get around now by renting a truck at Home Depot for only $50 for an entire day which allows me to transport massive amounts of goods. I also opened up one of those "first month free" storage locker deals so I don't have to hide my inventory in the woods and I can do business directly out of the storage unit.

I opened up a PO box at the local post office for only $25 for several months so now I have a real address I can use everywhere. After a month of busting my hump I managed to net and save up $2000. I know it isn't much but I came from nothing and now I have enough money to open up a checking account at the local bank. I am now drop shipping like crazy, I can sell products all month long without having to pay the eBay fees until the end of the month. I now buy and sell without limitations and I am tripling my money and I found a nice apartment with a roommate online, the apartment is in her name so I just pay her half the rent in cash every month.

I'm not homeless anymore, I even bought a new shirt and pair of pants to wear from the thrift store as my original shirt and pants were beginning to smell a bit as I hadn't taken a shower in months accept for once or twice in the fast food restaurant sink. Where do I go from here? Wherever I want!

While I have never been homeless, I have been bankrupted and penny less without a bank account or car and rebuilt my financial stability using the same methods. This was just one possible scenario, depending on location there may be other means of locating free inventory and different types of it. There are also many "We sell your stuff on eBay" stores popping up everywhere which also provides a means for income without actually having to have an eBay account. Alternatively, eBay offers a trading assistant program where you can search online to find someone local who will sell virtually anything of potential value for you free of initial charge. You could find a kid on there in his parents basement looking to make some extra money who is willing to sell anything and take a percentage of the total sales allowing you to generate revenue again free of charge and not contingent on your credit or having a bank account.

## College Student:

I am a full time college student; I live on campus in a

small dorm room unit with two other people and don't have any room for storing inventory or a means for shipping it out. Most of my day is spent in class and studying. I get a student loan check but after I pay for room and board and my classes I barely have enough left over to feed myself. It doesn't seem like I have many ways to generate a steady income other than getting a job at the University earning minimum wage and cutting into my needed study time. Plus I am in college! I should be worrying about parties, girls and living it up while I'm here, I can worry about money after I graduate. Well a little extra money wouldn't hurt, I have three hours of free time every day I guess I could use one of those hours to try and make some money.

Drop shipping seems like a viable way for me to make some money without cutting into my study or class time. It will also let me be lazy and not package things up and ship them out because that just seems like a hassle and I'm bored already just thinking about it. I remember reading that **www.ereselling.com** members have access to verified legitimate drop shipping companies with all their contact information provided and available products posted that I can resell.

I know that I don't need to have a tax id number to sign up for an account with all drop shippers but some require it. After registering for a tax id number for the IRS free of charge I can now have more options for opening accounts and if I start with a few smaller companies and establish a history with them I can use it as trade references to open up accounts with larger and more established companies in the future.

If I am going to make a consistent and profitable income from drop shipping I know that I need to find drop shippers that have clearly visible and routinely updated inventory lists. If I can download inventory updates daily or receive product quantity updates via e-mail I can ensure that my customers will receive the products they order from me and I don't have to cancel unavailable product orders.

I had to wait about a week but I have my tax id number and have successfully opened three drop shipper accounts. I have been researching different products that I can profitably resell and I have been using the free drop shipping calculator provided by **www.ereselling.com** to calculate my net revenue potential.

I setup an eBay store for selling the drop shipping items; I will also wait for promotions which run routinely on eBay for free auction listings. When I see this promotion I will send one of every item that I have in my eBay store to online auction. Over time if I continue this process I will be sending hundreds upon hundreds of products to online auction at once completely free of charge because I can keep reselling the same products over and over.

One of my biggest limitations with drop shipping is that I am getting hammered by a middle man, at least until I have the credit and capital and business standing to establish drop shipping accounts directly with manufacturers. The second concern I will face is beating the spread from selling on eBay, I will face commission fees up to 12% on some items and then additional fees when I receive the payment from. In many cases when selling on eBay I may only have a 20 to 30 percent profit margin with drop shipping if I'm lucky so that doesn't leave much left on the table. To automate my sales process on eBay as much as possible to free up as much as my time as I can I have signed up for eBay Blackthorne sales software. Blackthorne Basic is an all-in-one software application that will enable you to create professional listings in bulk, track the status of sales, and manage buyer communication and feedback - all from your desktop. Blackthorne Basic is ideal if you list at least 25 items a month and prefer an end-to-end desktop tool. It only cost me $10 a month and it will also allow me to relist unsold items in bulk. This software is a more advanced and feature oriented version of Turbo Lister.

To counteract the high commission fees on eBay I have setup an Amazon Pro Merchant store which costs me about $40 a month but saves me from paying the $.99 cent transaction fee from every sale on Amazon so I really only need to sell 40 items a month to make it profitable and I also have the ability now to create my own inventory page listings in the Amazon catalog which is searched by millions of customers a month. I have a variable commission rate that I will pay on successful sales on Amazon from 6 to 20 percent so my profit margin will vary. If a sale comes directly from Amazon my commission is much lower, if an Amazon Associate refers the sale of my product I will be hit with a higher fee so I need to make sure I mark my products at least 30% higher than I am drop shipping them for so I can be assured that I will never lose money.

My last sales marketplace will be one that I have created on my own using the free software Magento or OsCommerce which is very simple to install and detailed instructions for doing so and support are available on the distributor's websites. I purchased some very cheap Godaddy hosting at $3 a month by prepaying for six months in advance, normally it is $5 a month. I picked out a great domain name and registered it for less than $10 and uploaded and installed my new E-Commerce store in less than an hour. Once I add my products to my website I will be able to export my products to Google Shopping and Bing Shopping completely free of charge. This will allow users searching on either of those search engines for products similar to mine to see my products listed for sale. Users will click the items listed by the search engines and be directed directly to my sales page on my website. This will allow me to complete sales at a high volume free of charge.

After I have done the research and found products to sell for a profit I have 30 different products listed across eBay, Amazon and my personal website. Those are 30 different products and I have available drop shipping quantities of 20 of each individual product giving me a total sales potential of 600 total products. My average net profit after paying all the expenses for completing a sale is about $7 an item. Listing my products on three different marketplaces has allowed me to develop a net monthly income around $750. This is not a lot of money but I am a college student and I can handle this work load spending three hours a week or less fulfilling orders. In a few months when I have had time to increase my product catalog and have grown comfortable with my drop shippers and the process I will be able to handle a hundred different products spending no more than five hours a week. This will put my stable net income around $3000 a month, if I overload myself anymore than this I won't be able to keep up with school.

This was initially a very time consuming and experimental process. Many products did not sell well and I had to remove them from my catalog. Other products that I sold were not available by the time I went to place the order for my customer and I had to process many refunds. I stuck with it and every new product that I add from now on will add to my bottom line and eventually financial independence will be mine but I have to stay the course and not give up when I get frustrated with drop shipping.

## Full Time Jobs:

I work nine to five six days a week and I have three kids who play sports and will be going to college soon. I make a decent living but with the two cars, mortgage payment, car insurance, five cell phone bills, utilities and a mound of other expenses I don't have much left over after I get my pay check. If only I could earn another $10,000 a year I could relax a little bit more and not be so stressed out all the time. I just had to replace the transmission in my car and the dog's vet bills were several thousands of dollars. My savings account is basically tapped out and I don't know how I'm going to put three kids through college. I don't have the time to go to auctions and I certainly don't have time to package up and ship out merchandise to customers, I barely have time to brush my teeth in the morning. I do have a lot of time at work where I just sit and stare at my computer and that hour long lunch break, I wonder if I can make some extra money from those six hours I get for lunch a week and maybe add in a few hours on Sunday when I'm not running errands and taking the kids to their sports practice.

Come to think of it I remember learning about business liquidation auctions online. I can use AuctionZip to find companies that specialize in liquidation auctions but run the actual auction completely online so I don't have to physically be there to bid on items because who has time for that. They will also deliver the items to my house and if I purchase enough they will deliver it free.

I also can purchase pallets of wholesale goods from Liquidation.com and I remember that there is some site that is perfect for purchasing wholesale inventory from anywhere in the world with thousands upon thousands of verified and certified manufacturers and distributors. That's right, it was called Alibaba and I can search for products that I want to resell and match them with distributors and I can even chose which countries to include in my search results that I am willing to purchase from. I really love cars, especially the Mazda RX-8 and RX-7. Let me do a quick search to see if I can find anything related to them that I would be interested in purchasing. Well that is incredible, there are hundreds of different products I can buy including aftermarket exhaust systems, turbo units, sensors, decals, diecast model cars, key chains, T-shirts and so much more, I am overwhelmed!

I can use the market research tools that I have learned about to see how much I can resell these products for, I can also research the business liquidation inventory at the same time. After searching I realized that I can make a huge profit reselling the sensors, turbo units and model cars. I made sure that the market was not thin for these products, they have a sell through rate over 50% and I stand to make a profit of 75% on these items at the quoted price listed by the distributor. I want to order hundreds of each but I think I will play it safe and make sure the quality is good, reliability from the distributor is up to par and that I am able to resell them at the price I believe I can. I will contact each distributor and order a sample size order since mostly all wholesalers offer this service and if they don't I am not wasting my time or money on them. I will order ten of each item and not get carried away.

Time to bid on some business liquidation items, oh look they are liquidating a few restaurants, that is a shame but most restaurants don't make it more than a few years before going under so I bet this is fairly common. At these prices I can make at least three fold I think I'll bid on these meat slicers, coffee brewers, dough mixers and other goodies that are potential gold mines for my bottom line.

I got in way over my head, I won twenty auctions and they are large items. At least I got free delivery but I won't have time to take pictures and try to resell them and I sure won't have time to package and ship them out. Glad I found that local Trading Assistant on eBay's free platform who has a warehouse and specializes in restaurant and commercial supply. I can have the merchandise shipped directly to his warehouse and he will sell it for me, he even does freight shipping and only takes 30% of the sales price. I found three other auction companies in my area that specialize in online auctions, I can buy virtually any day of the week during my lunch break and forward the inventory to my new consignor and sit back and collect a check without getting my hands dirty.

I do have that other problem now, I ordered that wholesale inventory. The inventory is relatively small and since I purchased ten of each item I would only have to make one listing template for each individual item. Each item is new in box and packaging; I bet it would not be much work to ship out individual items I would just need to find the same size boxes for each item and time to print out shipping labels. Now that I think about it Uline has every size of box imaginable and they will even make custom sizes, I will setup an account with them right away so I can purchase boxes at wholesale prices. I can even set up my account so that if I keep selling the same products I can automate my box purchases and not have to worry about shipping supplies anymore. It would be so easy packaging and shipping these units since they will all have the same measurements and weighs over and over I wonder if my son could handle it. I could give him a little more allowance each week for helping me out, I am sure he would love to be a part of something and be glad to help out, maybe he will even learn something about business in the process.

The items arrived and two out of the three different types of products that I purchased were just what I expected and I made an even bigger profit than I had imagined, I think I will find some more of the same types of items to buy wholesale and the larger the quantity that I purchase the bigger the discount on price I get.

It has been a few months now and I have found many

different products that I enjoy selling and can flip for steady profits. I make one wholesale purchase a month, it takes me a few minutes online during my lunch break. It also takes me a few minutes to update my quantities on my online stores, I list them on my eBay store and I created an Amazon store where I created my own catalog page for each item I sell. Everything is virtually automated, my son handles the shipments and I sit back and collect the profits. I have also developed a great relationship with several online Trading Assistants and I have become a middle man where I purchase liquidation items at auction during my lunch break and basically sit back and wait for my check in the mail. I don't have to worry about putting my kids through college anymore and I didn't have to quit my job to start this little business up. Now that I think about it, I don't even need to go to my job anymore now that I can streamline this process my earning potential is limitless, but I will wait and see how things are after a year before I make any stupid decisions.

## Other Scenarios:

Most individuals will be able to use one of the preceding scenarios or a combination of them and apply it to generating income but there are a few other possibilities. For instance, I am good with a needle and thread but I am not a tech savvy individual and I can barely use a computer. Or I am great with my hands and work working but I'm not great with computers. I could get my grandson or son or brother to set me up an account with that site ETSY that I keep reading about. If I had an account with them I could sell my own handmade and crafted products on that site without much effort on my part. If I really don't feel like dealing with the internet to make sales I still have options. One of the simplest sales methods and easiest to manage is print advertising.

I can post free advertisements for the products that I am making and selling in the local newspaper, the local Penny Saver, coupon book mailer and I can even put up poster board ads on telephone poles and street corners as I would if I were having a yard sale. Come to think of it, having a yard sale is also another way of selling my products.

Keep in mind that you will have to answer phone calls and do business over the phone as well as have customers coming to your house on some occasions to purchase merchandise if you are not willing to package and ship items out or use e-mail.

If you can't make things and don't know how to use the internet in the most basic sense and you aren't willing to pursue any of the homeless person scenario strategies than you are in trouble my friend. You should put this book down and sign up for some training at a vocational school, university or buy some books at your local book store and educate yourself because you're in charge of your own life and if you don't have any useful skills or general technical knowledge it is your own fault for not investing in yourself and your future.

# <u>Chapter 8 – The Reseller Challenges</u>

I decided to take off from working the majority of the 2011 year to focus on going back and finishing up a college degree and to do some travelling and relaxing as well as work on this book. I have a few online blogs where I talk about different methods of selling online and generating revenue. I had several subscribers questioning that my abilities to generate such incomes that I had discussed from reselling products online and figured it was just hokum and I was trying to scam people out of their hard earned money. My sales accounts had been completely inactive as I had not been working in sometime. A few friends of mine noticed that I was sleeping in until one or two in the afternoon and spending the day watching TV, playing video games or otherwise being lazy and began to question my abilities. People often try to condemn me for sleeping in late and working only a few hours a week because they have to work 40 hour weeks and come off as very jealous of my work life. Others have implied that I am living a facade and putting on a front. As the long year of 2011 went on I found myself blowing through cash like I was a rock star and finally by the end of October I had some friends bet me that I couldn't make as much money as they do at their fancy jobs and it was time for me to give up on my dreams. Hearing this definitely awoke me from my comatose state and snapped my focus into over drive. I will not state what the stakes of the bet were but it wasn't for peanuts. Thus the "Reseller Challenge" was born. Following is my actual journal logs and status reports for the challenge.

# The $10,000 Profit in 30 Days Reseller Challenge

I am going to prove that ANYONE can make a living online; I plan on showing everyone how simple it is to make

$10,000 in a month. I am going to be using my cell phone for most of the challenge, that's right I am going to be armed only with my Motorola Bionic Droid, Market Research account and Handy Market app and whatever other apps or features of my phone I can use to meet the challenge. The reason I have accepted this challenge is simply to try and show that anything can be accomplished if you just get off the couch and apply yourself. I also want to prove to all the haters out there with the same old nine to five jobs that employment isn't always what it is cracked up to be.

## THE CHALLENGE:

I have to make a gross profit of $10,000 in 30 days with only a $3500 initial starting budget. I will have 30 days to buy, sell and ship out my inventory. I must accomplish this using sales channels and inventory sources that anyone can access without requiring a tax id, reseller license or corporation.

## CHANNELS FOR BUYING INVENTORY/SALES VENUES:

- **Purchases**: Estate Auctions, Estate Sales, Business Liquidations, Storage Auctions, Online Auctions, Wholesale Lots, Yard Sales and Thrift Stores.

- **Selling Venues:** eBay, Amazon, ETSY, Facebook Marketplace, Gunbroker, Classifieds/Forums, Local consignment auctions, my personal website bolky.com or another site that I create for this challenge.

## THE RULES:

- Must not exceed the budget of $3500

- Must complete buying and selling without hiring help or outsourcing tasks

- Must have an average hourly earnings rate of $100/hr when all said and done. This includes time spent purchasing inventory, driving to get or transport inventory as well as selling, customer support and shipping and handling of said inventory

- May not sell any previously owned inventory, properties or services.

- Must use only my cell phone for researching and purchasing but may use other means for listing, selling and shipping

- I may not spend $500 or more on any individual item

- Proof of income and expenses must be verified by a neutral third party

\* A crucial factor worth noting is that the main eBay account I will be using for the challenge is rather new and created for teaching, consulting and training purposes. It is faced with a $10,000 a month selling limit as per eBay's new seller policy.

# $10k Challenge – Day One – Nice Start!

The day started out nicely, I drove by two local thrift stores and quickly found, tested and purchased nine Hi-Fi VCR players. This is such a sleeper and one of my favorite quick flippers, over the last three years I've pushed $10k alone on VCRs spending less $500 on them. Both yard sales and thrift stores can yield massive ROI's and both allow bargaining if you know what you're doing. Anyway, since this is day one I will provide a little more details and some research of how I did below but I won't do that for every day as it took a lot of my time to do so. Here is a shot of what I grabbed from a local estate auction of a sports collector and also some items I picked up at the local thrift store:

Here are some photos:

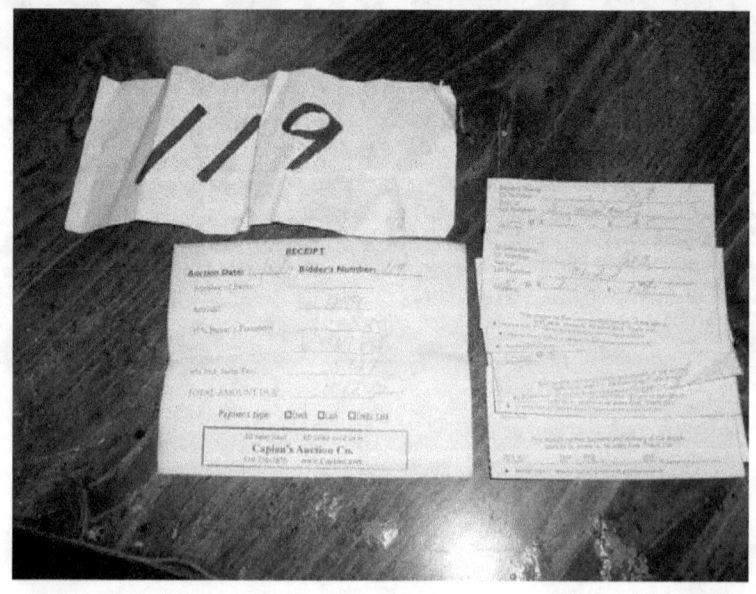

The massive lot of sports and event pennants includes some rare finds which should see some individual sales of upwards of $500. There are some rare collectible sports and board games that I found; several are valued at over $200 each. I was also able to pull out a stack of signed memorabilia free of charge given to me by the auctioneer for purchasing so many items. The VCRs will do very well on Amazon and my personal website and should see an average sales price of around $70 once I purchase the corresponding remote controls for them online which is very cheap and less than $10 for each. I purchased about fifty books for a measly $5 which should eventually sell for over $400 but most of which will not be collected by the end of this challenge. Books yield massive return on investment potential but typically have a thin market for collectible ones and take a decent amount of time to sell on average.

Total Spent Day One: $1,085

Total Estimated Gross Sales on inventory : $5,953

Day One Expected Gross Profit : $4868

Total hours spent day one (driving, bidding, driving, unloading) : 4.5 hours

# DAY TWO: $10k in 30 Days Challenge

Day two is in the books and I am a little bit worried about exceeding the established budget of only $3,500. Working with such a constricted budget and profit expectations from said budget does not leave me a lot of room for error and requires that I maximize my ROI to the fullest extent. This will mean that I have to start buying table lots and less value items that I can resell for a much higher return on investment than is usually returned with more valuable items. Since I cannot buy an individual item for $500 and resell it for $2000 under the terms of the challenge I am going to work on a slightly different strategy but I am still very optimistic that I will reach my target profit of $10k in 30 days.

I went to one of my favorite auctions on day two and had to take a more passive stance, usually I would be aggressive and run items up in price and purchase $200 items that I can resell for $500 but that strategy would simply not work for this challenge. After a very strong day one and an expected almost 5 to 1 return on my money I ended up buying items that I can maybe pull off a 3 to 1 return as there was intense and fierce competition that I had a hard time laying down too and found myself in a few bidding wars and paying too much for certain items. It can definitely go a long way if you make an example in the beginning of an auction that you won't be bullied around and you have money and you're a serious player but it can be costly sometimes as well. I learned this principal a few years back when I was a semi-professional poker player. It can be better to be feared and respected sometimes than loved.

If I am going to successfully hit my target I will certainly need to focus on ROI, this will lower my hourly rate for certain and should make things very interesting because I won't be able to crush this challenge as I originally thought. Mentally If I needed to make a quick $10k I would go out and spend $10k and just double it which is far easier and faster when only purchasing a few high ticket items. As it currently stands I am playing this one to close to the chest and with a maximum net profit of $6k and over half my budget spent already I will fail if I keep up this pace. The key factor is that it is all "potential" profits and with only 30 days to work with I will not be able to unload 100% of the items for maximum profit. This will end up forcing me to send items to auctions; both online and locally towards the end of the time period which will kill profits, things just got a bit interesting!

In order to maximize profits I am going old school and not paying for any packaging or materials but gathering them from local shopping outlets and anywhere else I can locate them. I will also be adding a nice handling fee and boosting shipping costs a tiny fraction so that if I sell 150 items with a hidden average profit in shipping of $5 I can add an additional $750 to my bottom line. Obviously I am not going to do this on items that weigh a pound or two, but the larger items I can squeeze in profits of $10-$20 sometimes which I usually would then in turn outsource for shipment but I will be pocketing every penny I can and doing it myself.

In order to keep the highest hourly rate I showed up for the auction right as it started at 6:00 PM armed only with my cell phone and was out by 7:00 (usually I would recommend arriving at least a minimum of an hour ahead of time so you can properly do research and test/inspect any items before bidding).

Here is a shot at what I picked up on day two, spending $512

My estimated figures thus far:

Total Spent Day Two: $512

Estimated Gross Resale Value: $1650

Estimated Gross Profit: $1139

Total time spent Day Two: 2.5 hours

Total Challenge Time Spent: 7 hours

Total Challenge Spending: $1597

Total Challenge Potential Resale Value: $7603

Total Challenge Potential Gross Profit: $6006

**DAY THREE: $10k in 30 Days Challenge**

This was an extremely productive day! The day started off early in the morning and I was able to test, research and get pictures of all 128 items that I had picked up in days one and two. This took me three hours to complete this part of the daily process and three Red Bulls.

I was able to set a few personal best for the day; I listed 128 items for sale from scratch in a single day! The listing process took me five and half hours multi tasking like crazy and zipping through listings.

- Listed 81 items in Turbo Lister for eBay Auctions/Stores – I hit my monthly $10k listing/selling limit on eBay which will add a few more challenges my way.

- Listed 42 items on Amazon

- Listed 3 items on GunBroker

- Listed 2 items on CraigsList

Now that day three is complete and I have listed all of the products from days one and two it is time to go find some more inventory! I will be on the lookout for storage auctions this time and business liquidations, if I can find a nice auction of either this challenge will certainly be a lock ☻

Total Challenge Time Spent Day Three: 8.5 hours

Total Challenge Time Spent: 15.5 hours

Total Challenge Spending: $1597

Total Challenge Potential Resale Value: $7603

Total Challenge Potential Gross Profit: $6006

# DAY Four: $10k in 30 Days Challenge

I wanted to hit up a storage auction or two but could not find any decent ones in my area. Storage units are usually held at the beginning and ends of the month by most companies. This challenge has started and will end in the middle of the month so I may have to wait a few weeks before the bulk of the storage auctions in my area are held and it may just be to late by then. My preference with storage auctions is that they be within ten miles from my warehouse. If I have to rent a truck because I got a trashy storage unit it would get ridiculously pricey running back and forth to the local dump.

I was out running errands and I decided to type in "thrift" into my GPS and found two thrift stores I had not been to before. I spent $100 on the dot between the two thrift stores and purchased many items I can list on Amazon since my eBay account is currently over the limit (I will most likely start using one of my other eBay accounts if need be).

It only took me an hour and a half to get to the stores, make my purchases and bounce out. I knew exactly what I was looking for and didn't stop moving or browse for anything else. It took me another hour to complete the testing and taking of pictures of the items. I listed most of the items on Amazon in a matter of minutes as the listing process is so sweet and simple it only takes a matter of seconds for each listing.

Pictures of Day Four Thrift Store Pickups:

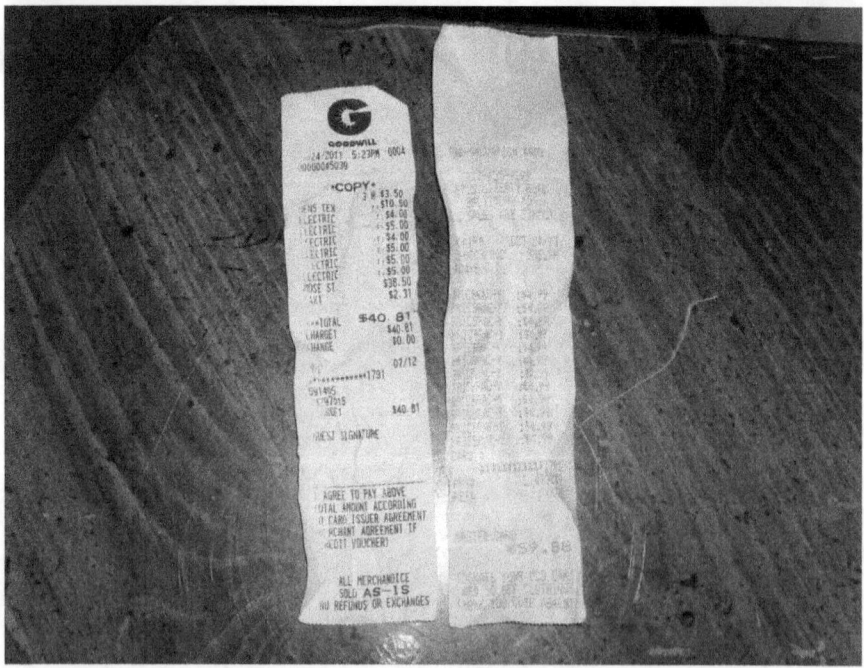

(I was able to get some items free since I negotiated and purchased so many items – the receipt is missing a few items)

I almost forgot I went by my local Hallmark store and picked up some packaging FREE (may hold me over for a few days):

Potential Resale Value of 19 VCRS (listing on Amazon mostly): $1129

Potential Resale Value of other thrift store pickups: $525

Potential Day Four Potential Sales: $1654

Day four Time Spent: 3 hours

eBay Gross Sales in 4 Days: $660

Amazon Gross Sales in 4 Days: $229

Total Challenge Time Spent: 18.5 hours

Total Challenge Spending: $1697

Total Challenge Budget Remaining: $1803

Total Challenge Potential Resale Value: $9257

Total Challenge Potential Gross Profit: $7560

Total Challenge Current Sales (As of Day four) : $889

## DAY Five: $10k in 30 Days Challenge

This was mostly a recover and be lazy day, I slept in till about 2:00PM and watched TV and movies most of the day. I shipped out 9 very small items that took less than an hour. I also copied about 50 listings from eBay and Amazon to Bolky.com. I blasted my customer list on Bolky of about 2500 customers of collectibles and past sales to let them know about the new products I just got in. By the end of the night I sold 13 pennants, 7 VCRs, 11 boxes of sealed baseball cards and five sports games. The total gross sales off of that I have not yet added up but will include it in my weekly update.

This is also kind of cheating but not really, I went to a local free book exchange (open two days a week – take as many as 150,000 books free) and grabbed five boxes filled to the top with FREE books that will all sell on Amazon. I used my cell phone with an app known as Handy Market which allows me to scan barcodes and instantly bring me to the sales page on Amazon to see what the sales ranking and current market price is for said item. At the end of week one I will add the total Amazon potential sales into account of potential resale value.

Total Time Spent Day Five: 3 hours

Total Challenge Time Spent: 21.5 hours

Total Challenge Spending: $1697

Total Challenge Budget Remaining: $1803

Total Challenge Potential Resale Value: $9257

Total Challenge Potential Gross Profit: $7560

Total Challenge Current Sales (As of Day four) : $889

# DAY SIX: $10k in 30 Days Challenge

I went back to the estate auction for the sports memorabilia, they have been having two sales a week since there is so much inventory to liquidate. I was hoping to spend the remaining budget I have left and knock this challenge out of the park but I was only able to spend $524. I ran into some collectors that I couldn't shake, I ran them up several thousands of dollars over a period of a few items but they wouldn't back down or off so I was not able to get the prime merchandise I was hoping for. At this point it didn't make sense to overpay for items just to make a point as that would certainly have helped my image and pride but not help me win this challenge.

Total time spent to and from the auction: 3.5 hours

Total spent at the estate auction: $524

Estimated Potential Resale Value: $2650

Here is a shot of some of the goodies I got at the auction:

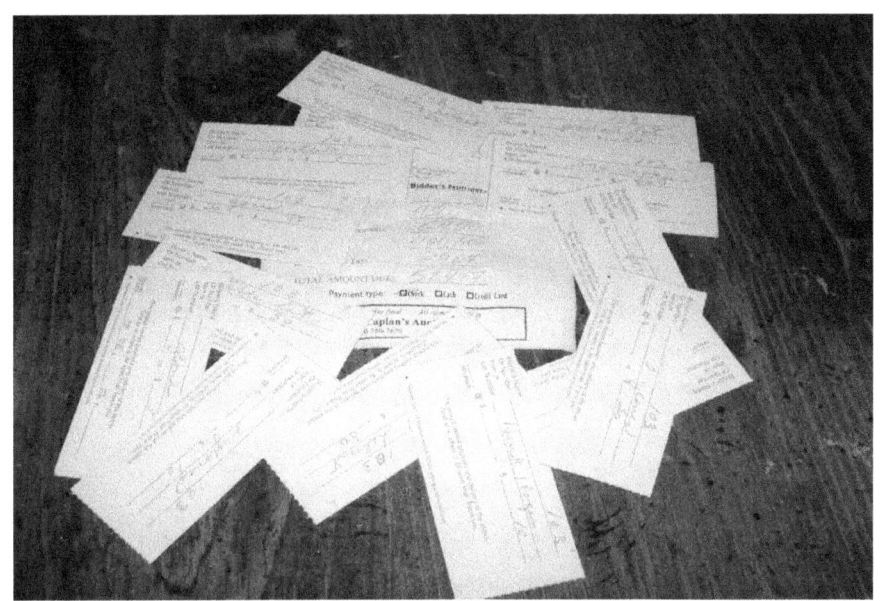

Total Challenge Time Spent: 25 hours

Total Challenge Spending: $2221

Total Challenge Budget Remaining: $1279

Total Challenge Potential Resale Value: $11907

Total Challenge Potential Gross Profit: $9686

Total Challenge Current Sales (As of Day four) : $889

# DAY SEVEN: $10k in 30 Days Challenge

I spent most of the time today driving around making sales; I went by my local sports collectible shop and was able to make a fairly nice deal. I sold 21 boxes of sealed baseball cards, five pennants, one of the World Series rings from yesterday's auction, a glove and a signed sports book for $550. I went to a few music shops but was only able to sell one guitar for $75, they tried to butcher me on the others so I bounced out of there. I went down the street to a strip of antique shops and sold a black powder pistol and a medieval sword from the same auction and another one of the antique baseball gloves for a total of $575. This process of driving around and selling took me close to three hours. Luckily for me they were all within ten miles of my house so I definitely saved some time there.

I spent the rest of the time shipping out 42 items that had sold on Bolky.com, Direct sales from my E-mail list, Amazon and eBay. Being a little bit rusty shipping items out it took me longer than I had expected and I actually worked a full day today as shipping took me four hours to complete! I miss paying to have my items packaged and shipped but sometimes you got to just bear down and do whatever is needed.

Since the eBay account used for this challenge is capped I will have to think outside the box for a lot of the selling and besides eBay is overrated. If you are relying on one place, one method or one means of sales than you are truly limiting your potential profits and putting your sales future in jeopardy. If that one vendue that you rely on goes under than your financial future may be at stake. You will see I can make a lot more money and faster selling to past customers and on my own but it is a great way to dump items and recover some capital but you won't get maximum value in most cases. Next week I intend on selling on Facebook Marketplace and Gunbroker to bring in some more gains and increase exposure for my listings.

Total Time Spent Day Seven: 7 hours!

Total Challenge Time Spent: 32 hours

Total Challenge Spending: $2221

Total Challenge Budget Remaining: $1279

Sales totals and updates are coming in the Week One update next!

# WEEK ONE: $10k in 30 Days Challenge

It was not the best week ever but it's a start, I still have a nice chunk of my budget left so hopefully I can find a nice storage unit and flip it (my best ROI on a storage unit was $45 spent and $13700 profit) or maybe a nice juicy business liquidation or if I'm lucky I might go to an auto auction and flip a car or truck for a nice profit. Oh and did I mention that I am taking 18 credits in college finishing a degree I started 10 years ago so I am doing all of this while maintaining a 3.8 GPA 😊

This is an update for the total week one activity and progress report.

Total Items Listed on Amazon: 229 – value: $4972

Total eBay items listed: 142 – value: $8632

Unlisted items + Day six items potential resale value: $3152

Gross Sales Totals – Week One – $4838

- eBay Sales : $853

- Amazon : $497

- Bolky.com + Collectors E-Mail list: $1851

- Sports Trading Card Shop: $550

- Antique Dealer Shops: $575

- Music Store: $75

- Craigslist: $310

- Estate Auction Sales: $127

Total Challenge Time Spent: 32 hours

Total Challenge Spending: $2221

Total Challenge Budget Remaining: $1279

Total Challenge Gross Sales: $4838 (Does not reflect any profit/loss from shipping & handling)

Total Challenge Gross Profit (Week One): $2617

Total Challenge Current Inventory Potential Resale Value: $16,756.00

## DAY 16: $10k in 30 Days Challenge – OVER!

Sorry everyone for the delay catching you up, I got very lucky and hit up a Storage Auction and an Estate auction that virtually nobody was at and basically had my way with anything I wanted. That wasn't the kicker though, I found something that many people would perhaps overlook but I had sold in the past for ridiculous profits. They are very rare to come by so don't expect to just go to your local yard sale or thrift store and pick them up. What am I talking about? Uncut trading card sheets, baseball, football, basketball and even garbage pail kids to name a few of the ones I've sold – more so the vintage sheets 1960-1980 from my experience on the big money ones. Since I had sold some before in the past (four of the same ones I got this time for $650 each) the collector who purchased them is a very wealthy doctor in California and begged me to contact him if I ever ran across anymore.

I might have found a few at this auction....58 SHEETS! To be exact and I picked up the phone immediately and left a message. After some negotiating I decided to cut him a deal so I could go on vacation for a few weeks (why this blog had not been updated for awhile) and I sold him 24 of the sheets he was interested in for only $7200 (That is only $300 each, I have sold them for as much as $650 each but wholesaling for quick cash never hurts), but that was enough to put me over the top. I have not added up all the other sales yet but the 30 day total will be very impressive....oh and I purchased all the sheets for only $210....($125 was spent on just two of the sheets the others were bundled from $5 to $10).

Here is what they look like, the ones I have left (should be close to $10k in leftover inventory at least) I just snapped a shot of in case you have the pleasure of running across them:

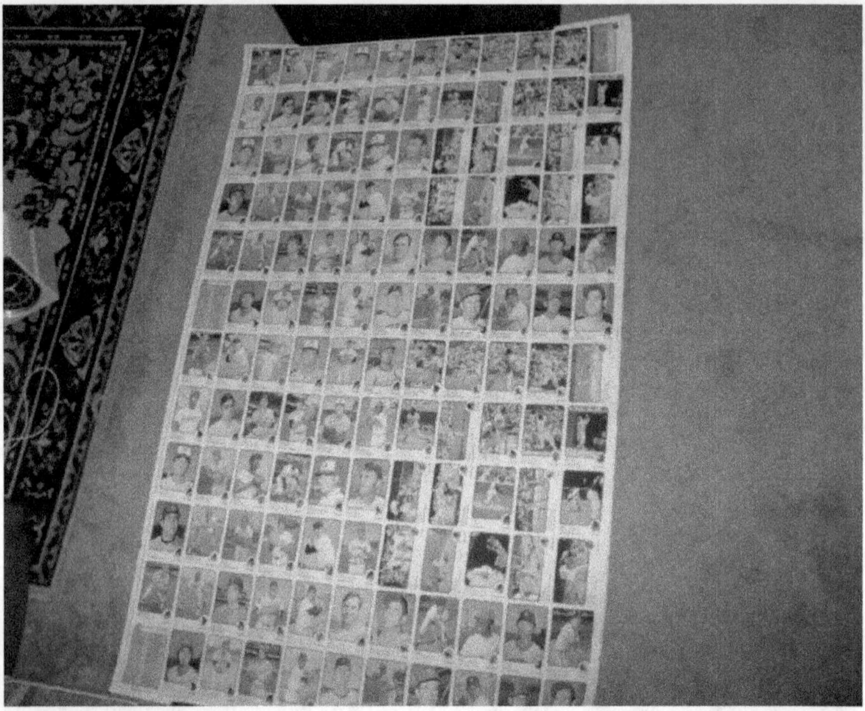

Here were a few more inventory purchases that I did for the challenge from a storage auction unit and estate sale (I was basically stealing – this was all for under $1000!)

Please note: Revenue totals and Sales online include those items from The Reseller Challenge and do not include sales from my other eBay/Auction/Marketplace accounts, do not include domain name parking revenues, domain name sales, website sales, website product and service sales or advertising and referral monthly revenues accrued by ByteCash Media LTD during this 30 day time period.

I am sorry that this challenge was not more "challenging" and I did not have a chance or the need to post status updates as it was a very quick $10k+.

I completed the first reseller challenge which was to earn $10k profit in one month buying and reselling inventory throughout online marketplaces and venues. I really did not need to use many sources as I said in my last update that I had hit a homerun with the uncut trading card sheets which accounted for $7200 alone. After I made that sale I really kind of felt bad because I made this all look too easy but the point is, if you apply yourself and take calculated risk and get off the couch once in awhile good things can and will happen. In the past I have had monthly profits of $53,400 – $38,291 – $31,229 – $27,478 to name a few of my record months and that was mostly due to putting myself in the right places at the right times. For instance, I had acquired on consignment a lot of about 5,000 original National Geographic Canvas Map prints (many duplicates) from the very beginning of National Geographic with the negatives used to create them and had one individual collector pay $33k and another $7k for some bulk purchases and made over $1k a day selling the rest online at 50% commission per sale.

One of the problems I had with this specific challenge was that the eBay account that I setup to use for this site and for general education/teaching/experimenting and was created last year so it was limited to selling and listing $10k worth of inventory a month. I do have a main eBay account but was not going to use it as deciphering drop ship sales and other merchandise from this challenge would have been a nightmare. I did however use a backup account that I used to complete a few sales but only totalling $1144.

The journal entries and picture taking was halted when I reached my target sales goal, it was reached in less than 20 days into the challenge. That did not mean that sales stopped coming in and I shut down all my accounts and closed my listings. During the next ten days many more sales would pour in and I have gone back and revised the true sales totals for the 30 day period as to reflect upon the true outcome. It is also worth noting that from that same inventory I would continue a high rate of sales for the next several months after which was completely 100% profit.

CHALLENGE GROSS TOTALS:

Direct Buyer of 24 Uncut Trading Card Sheets: $7200

Total Items Listed on Amazon : 254

Total Gross Sales on Amazon : $1360

Total eBay items listed: 239

Total eBay Sales: $8340

Bolky.com Direct Website Sales: $711

Bolky.com Collectors Mailing List: $1427

Facebook Marketplace: $700 (One bulk purchase from one buyer – large lot of the sports pennants)

Gunbroker: $224

Sports Trading Card Shop: $550

Antique Dealer Shops: $575

Music Store: $75

Craigslist: $310

Estate Auction Sales: $127

TOTAL 30 DAY GROSS RESELLER SALES: $21,599

TOTAL 30 DAY SPENDING: $3107

TOTAL 30 DAY TIME SPENT: 84 HOURS (Buying, Listing/Promoting, Shipping/Dropping off)

TOTAL 30 DAY GROSS HOURLY EARNINGS: $257/HOUR

## Sales and Traffic  Learn more

Orders Placed x   Sessions x

423%
317%
211%
106%
0%

| /14 | Nov 15 | Nov 16 | Nov 17 | Nov 18 | Nov 19 | Nov 20 | Nov 21 |

2010

View: By Day | By Week | By Month

Export  ∨   Pivot  ∨

| | Date | Ordered Product Sales | Units Ordered |
|---|---|---|---|
| | 11/28/2011 | $30.96 | 2 |
| | 11/29/2011 | $9.98 | 1 |
| | 11/30/2011 | $0.00 | 0 |
| | 12/01/2011 | $10.98 | 1 |
| | 12/02/2011 | $77.96 | 2 |
| | 12/03/2011 | $0.00 | 0 |
| | 12/04/2011 | $29.86 | 2 |
| | 12/05/2011 | $12.48 | 1 |
| | 12/06/2011 | $37.96 | 2 |
| | 12/07/2011 | $30.48 | 1 |
| | 12/08/2011 | $45.96 | 2 |
| | 12/09/2011 | $0.00 | 0 |
| | 12/10/2011 | $48.44 | 3 |
| | 12/11/2011 | $91.18 | 2 |
| | 12/12/2011 | $79.45 | 1 |
| | 12/13/2011 | $86.40 | 4 |
| | 12/14/2011 | $120.77 | 5 |
| | 12/15/2011 | $29.86 | 2 |
| | **Total** | **$1,360.10** | **47** |

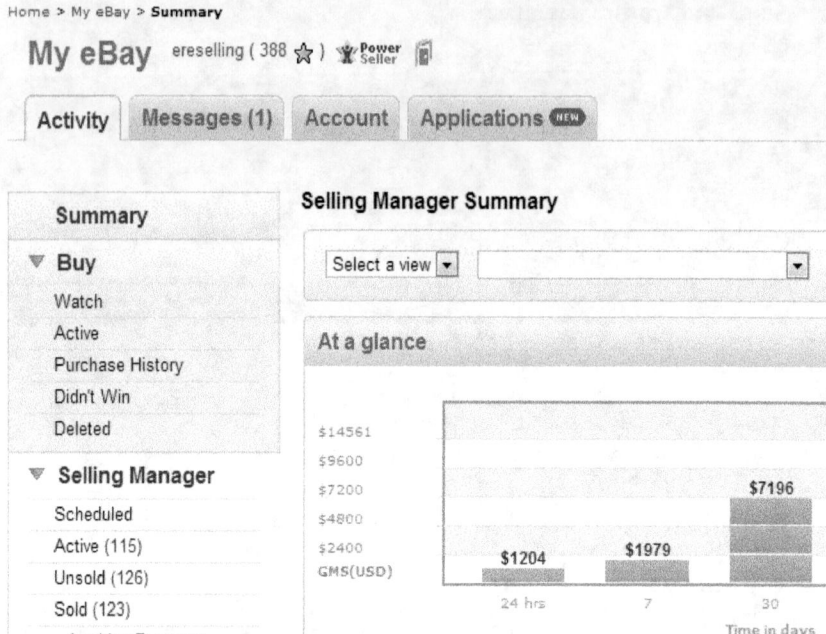

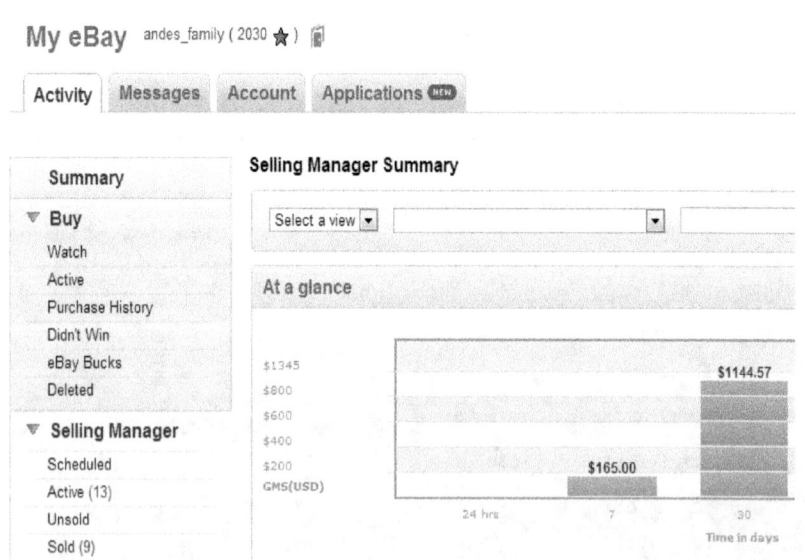

For a more detailed analysis of the strategies used to buy and sell these products and create such revenues I have added some online videos of tasks and strategies can be viewed at **ereselling.com**

My typical hourly rate from reselling is usually between $75-$100/hour so these results are not typical – just a great month where I applied myself and had some luck!

Keep in mind that I have only posted gross sales results, it is obvious that the net sales was over the challenge and the people involved in the challenge know the exact figures but a complete breakdown of commissions, fees, charges and expenses would consume unwarranted space here.

# Chapter 9 - Final Thoughts

## Perseverance & Will

Throughout my business travels and experiences I have met all kinds of different people from geniuses and morons to the apathetic and the driven. The world needs both lambs and shepherds so there is nothing wrong with settling for a "normal" work a day life. Studies have shown that entrepreneurs on average are more satisfied with their lives and overall happier people than those who have normal jobs. If you want to become something more, I encourage you to venture out and stake your claim.

Fortune will always favour the bold, but being bold will require the will and heart to persevere. In life the one who wants it more will get it, I have known so many highly educated and highly intelligent people that end up doing nothing with their lives, too scared to take a calculated risk, too scared to fail and end up living mediocre unfulfilling lives giving nothing back to society and a legacy that will die with them. I am not knocking on college, personally I just went back to finish up a degree that I left off ten years ago to pursue a business. I think an education is needed for success but that does not mean a college education, self-education can be far more valuable. If you are going to college do it for the right reasons, for an education and to learn, not to get a degree so you can get a job. Albert Einstein was a C student, he suffered from ADHD, he would say he was blessed with ADHD. There is a genius inside all of us! Believe in yourself!

## Learn to delegate authority! Build Passive Income!

I am talking about self-employed people especially but this also pertains to small business owners as well. What is the most valuable asset in life? TIME! Yes money is valuable as well but having more free time provides us the opportunity to create more money, expand a business, venture into new markets and sit back and plan the future of your endeavour. If your too busy working 15 hours a day being self employed trying to make as much money as you can you're going to burn out eventually. Being self-employed is great but if you don't work do you still get paid? If you got sick or injured and couldn't work for the unforeseeable future how long would you last before you ran out of money?

The first company I ran I was about 20 years old when I started it with some buddies and we had an eBay business and a massive warehouse with loads of consignment contracts, we got real estate foreclosure deals and liquidated all the assets on eBay, we got this one deal from the Smithsonian which included 50 massive bins that we were filled with thousands of canvas maps, original prints and the negatives to make all of the National Geographic Maps and books. We started selling them on eBay and our websites and built up a client base, I was selling about $2000 worth a day at one point but I was also working 20 hours a day and pulling all nighters. I made around $20k a month for doing grunt work of taking pictures, writing descriptions, shipping out items but I lost focus of the business itself. I had to turn away consignment contracts, expansion opportunities, I was so caught up in the quick money that when the maps finally ran out I was right back where I started, well I had a nice bank account but the business had gone nowhere. Looking back on that time, I was afraid to let anyone else do the simple job of selling maps and I put myself into self-employed mode and not business owner mode. I could have easily hired any college kid, work at home mom or person off the street and paid them $10/hr to list these maps and that would had freed up four months of my life and provided me with passive income. I could have hired two or three people to do the job and instead of having $60k I would of had $50k and four months of my life back! Used that time to hire more employees, create more business contracts and after the four months had ten times as much inventory, more employees and closer to financial freedom even if my bank account was empty at that point it. It would start growing more rapidly with more contracts and employees and my work load goes down and down and income goes up and up and the climb out of the rat race begins….

Yes I know there is the old adage…never pay somebody to do something you can do yourself….try running a business that way…let me know where you end up in five years

I eventually did learn to delegate, and hired college kids to ship out packages, another college kid to answer the phones and handle e-mails and customer relations. I hired someone to go find deals for me, someone to handle the accounting, etc. During that time I found myself with nothing left to do, If I did not show up for work it didn't matter anymore I was still getting paid. Finally I was not self-employed anymore and I was a business owner, I could jump back out of the work cycle and it flowed without me being involved which led me to expand the company and take it off but that's another story after that…

Today I am self-employed, but I work like a business owner. At any given time I have about 20 or so websites under my media company ranging from E-Commerce sites, forums, blogs, membership sites, etc and there is no way I can manage them all and keep them updated and flowing. There is no way I can drop ship products, handle customer complaints, list items on eBay, write blog posts, go to auctions and buy products, ship out hundreds of items a week. I act like a business owner with twenty employees, but instead I hire freelancers, contractors and other businesses to do the work for me. You can do this too! I don't care what business you're in you can use some help! You will never leave the rat race if you stay self-employed.

Here are some examples of tasks I have outsourced:

- I've paid college kids $8/hr to ship out physical items I've sold. I charged a small handling fee on everything that was to be shipped out which left a small profit in the actual shipping cost and what the customer paid. The difference can be used to fund outside help without killing profits, it should actually boost them because you will be free to find and sell more inventory.

- I've paid accountants to keep track of the books – enough said here! Numbers can be boring.

- Hired marketing firms and website promotion companies to handle link building, search engine traffic placement, and keywords to drive sales to my websites.

- I have webmasters install PHP scripts, write bits of code to make sites more ascetically pleasing, designing banners, icons and logos.

- I constantly bid out projects on freelance sites a few good ones that you can get away with having a smaller budget on are ones such as **vWorker** or **Scriptlance**. **elance** is also good but there are a lot of bigger companies and hiring price tags for projects on that site.

By outsourcing unimportant tasks like these I can focus on more important matters like selling a small web business or buying one, creating new business relationships, planning the future – DON'T GET STUCK DOING THE SAME THING DAY IN AND DAY OUT! Open your eyes! There is a better way to live.

Regardless of what you are selling, whether it is physical or drop ship products, domain names, websites, eBooks or other digital content there will be one thing in common – customer information. This is a huge asset to you and your business and you should create a database or spreadsheet to keep track of this information. If you are physically send a product to a customer you should include a business card, flyer, discount coupon or something else that can bring the customer back to your website, eBay/Amazon/ETSY or other store. It can be kind of a gray area with spam but you can create a mailing list both e-mail and physical mail and send customers coupons, discounts and promotions about your related products or services that they purchased from you. Just make sure your not spamming their inbox's and mailboxes with junk and always use an e-mail manager that will allow the customer to "opt-out" of your e-mail list, if you provide this option and they opt-out do not continue sending them mail or you may set yourself up for a lawsuit. It is also common practice to sell customer information to third parties either to advertise to them or add them to their sites in an acquisition and customer information can be extremely valuable. Typical valuations can range from a few cents a customer to fifty dollars or more. When Myspace was sold the customer valuation was reported to be $38 per customer! So depending on what your product line or service line is your customers may be your most valuable asset.

If you have decided to make some financial changes in your life and invest your hard earned money and priceless time into your new venture I applaud you. It may be very frustrating at first and at times it may seem hopeless. If that happens then you will have to dig down deep and find the strength to keep pushing forward. You can never fail if you never give up trying, you will only become a failure if you quit trying. Yes, you may be "failing" but that is how human beings learn some of their most important lessons, just make sure you learn from your mistakes and not make the same ones over again.

So you made your first attempt to start a company or become self-employed to venture out on your own with unwavering confidence but something went wrong and your venture failed. You had staked so much money into it, countless hours and you blood sweat and tears when needed. You had to such pride, you were taking the road less travelled and blazing your own path. You didn't need to answer to anybody because you were on top of the world and you dictated your own life now. When people would call you arrogant you would tell them it was just confidence and maybe they needed some of their own. Over time you had been so caught up in your business that you lost sight of your personal life, maybe pushed a few friends away and maybe hurt the ones that love you. Maybe you put on an extra pound or two or maybe 30 and lost touch with the rest of the world. Ok, I am obviously talking about myself and what happened to me, but I know I am not alone at least on some accounts.

Being so young when I first became successful didn't help either, at the age of 21 I was running a company while all my friends were still in college and living with their parents. I was driving a new sports car, eating lobster dinners, meeting with executives and important people while my friends were worried about mid-terms and finals. That didn't help to deflate my ever expanding ego. So when failure finally comes and you have been living your life as though you were invincible and impervious to failure how do you react? Maybe people had been waiting on the sidelines for you to fail and now they want to stick it in your face, and maybe you deserved it. Maybe you had to move back home with your parents and borrow their car to go out because yours was repossessed. Maybe you don't have your 100k credit line anymore as a safety net. Maybe nobody was there to pick you up when you fell because you had pushed them all away.

People say "it's not where you've been but it's where you're going that matters". That statement I feel is really only half true, the places we've been and the experiences we've been through are what make us who we are. Once you have been through the right experiences and situations it can fuel where you're headed in life. If you have never failed at anything you'll be much more unlikely to truly succeed at anything. When I was just 20 years old (2002) I started my first company without any formal business experience, business training or education and no financing for that matter. What did matter was where I was going but since I had not yet run a business before I was unaware of all that goes into it. Three years later the business finally went under but myself and the co-founders had grown the company to the point where it had acquired two smaller businesses, a board of directors, multiple eBay drop-off locations, employees and a 50,000 sq ft warehouse full of inventory which literally burned to the ground and slowly became the cancer that would eventually kill the company with debt, loss of employees and so on.

I must have failed a thousand times in my first business experience but my will was not finally broken until I lost everything. Some people would not be eager to start another business and get back out there, I was one of those people and I shut down completely. For a solid year after this experience I was broken and had to move back in with my parents and slept twelve hours a day and stayed in bed for another four being too scared to get back on my feet and face the day. I had such a negative outlook on life that I felt like anything I did from now on I would fail at. I had burned all my bridges with business contacts and friends and felt chained down. It wasn't until two cousins of mine saved my life, both of them needing money sought to learn about selling online. This finally awoke me from my lifeless comatose state and lit a fire back in me that still burns to this day to never want to be a failure again.

So how do you overcome failure?

History is not paved with the memories of those who failed and gave up, their names have long been forgotten. The first step is to take responsibility for your failure. It's easy to point fingers and blame the world for your problems and those around you. I blamed the people who stole a car and burned my warehouse to the ground, I blamed my ex-girlfriend for wanting to spend so much time with me, instead of letting me work, I blamed all of my business partners for not doing their parts and making them feel like I had to do everything. I was a coward, a 23 year old coward who could not take responsibility for failing.

One of the problems that I didn't know how to deal with was "failure". I was always very good at sports, games and anything competitive and didn't know how to lose. Until this time in my life I considered myself a financial guru. People twice my age would ask me for retirement advise, investing advise, real estate advice and so forth. Being surrounded by CEOs, entrepreneurs, investors and millionaires for the last several years I couldn't imagine having to crawl back to my old friends and social group. Having lived at the top of the ladder and then slipping to fall all the way to the ground I now can understand why failed businessmen and those who fall from grace can take their own lives. I deserved it; having thought anything I touched would turn to gold and people were privileged to be in my presence is certainly no way to live your life.

Leaders need to be able to inspire those around them and give orders to others and it can be easy to get lost inside that character. You will be nothing without those around you that support you and hold you up, it is a symbiotic relationship. Please make sure on your way up the ladder that you keep things in perspective, you stop to enjoy time with your family, your friends and anyone meaningful in your life. Be confident in your abilities and what you are pursuing but certainly don't make others feel inferior.

Finally I realized after being humbled to the ground that I was responsible for everything that had befallen me. I should have made sure that the company was properly insured and would cover the damages and cost of the inventory that literally went up in flames. My ex-girlfriend was just trying to be a good girlfriend. Having someone love you, make every meal for you, support you right or wrong and just simply want to spend every waking hour with you is something that can't be taken for granite. If you have to work and have to take care of business, do it but make time for the ones who love you or you will have nobody to share your success with.

After you have taken responsibility, forgive yourself! This can be a hard thing to do, I punished myself, I locked myself away from the world and spent countless sleepless nights trying to find reasons to go on living. Face your mistakes, face your failures, don't abuse yourself or your self-esteem will go out the window. Say "I failed, but I also learned how not to run a business, how not to live my life and next time around I will make adjustments and changes so it doesn't happen again".

After you have taken responsibility and forgiven yourself you are ready to study your failure and learn from it. Analyse exactly what went wrong, what you did when it went wrong and contemplate ideas of what you could have done differently and what you will do differently next time around. Be confident in knowing you can make it work and believe that you will have another chance at success. Take "I can't" and "I don't know how" out of your vocabulary. I had a rule with my employees, they couldn't tell me that they couldn't do something or they didn't know how to do a task. I made them learn and figure out how to do it. Every day it gets easy to self-educate thyself, with Smartphone's and blazing fast and accessible internet access there is no excuse. You have access to such a mass of information, learn something new every day. Success is a habit and so is failure so train yourself to never give up, to figure things out and find answers and it will be as habitual as brushing your teeth.

Spend time with your friends and family, get back to childhood happiness. Surround yourself with POSITIVE people and successful and ambitious individuals. If you let negative people into your life they will drain your spirits and kill your "can do" attitude. Build a network of business associates that share similar goals. Find a mentor, someone who can keep you balanced, motivated and reassure you when times are tough.

Don't let arrogance get in the way of learning and growing, trust me you don't know everything and you don't have all the answers. If you get complacent and stop learning you will fall behind, be open to knowledge as it can come from unexpected sources. Study your competitors and those who have been successful in your business, don't assume they can't beat you and you're too smart and don't need any help being successful.

Don't be afraid to make mistakes again, this is a common theme that I see happen a lot. People fail once, lose money somewhere and they don't have the courage to try it again and take risks. In life you have to be willing to take risks and chances, if you are not willing to risk anything you're not going to gain anything. Get out of your comfort zone, do things you wouldn't normally do, be adventurous. Don't try and predict the future, CREATE IT!

Remember, always be legit! You can only scam people so many times before you end up in jail, your reputation is destroyed and you have to move on to another scam – it will never end. "It takes 20 years to build a reputation and five minutes to ruin it. If you think about that, you'll do things differently" - Warren Buffett

I have provided you on the next page with a list of sites that have been discussed within this book and services. The ones that have a .ereselling.com extension on the end may include a more detailed overview of some of the services and features offered for that site.

## Many Thanks & Best Wishes!

# USEFUL RESOURCES & LINKS

**www.ereselling.com** – A membership site that I created that provides customers with online video tutorials on how to buy and sell online. Also includes a drop shipper and wholesalers list to get started. There are product manuals with howto's on building and creating products that you can resell and much more, it is routinely updated with content.

## Buying Wholesale and Drop Shipping Companies

**Dropshipping.ereselling.com** – World Wide Brands is my FAVORITE Drop Shipping & Wholesale company directory that I have used. I have used this company's service since 2002 and it offers the biggest list of verified drop shippers with over 8,000 companies currently in their database, they are the easiest to use and most reliable company I have come across. You can search for products that you would like to sell and their database will match the products to the company. The benefit of this is that you can apply to hundreds of companies in a matter of minutes, all your information is stored in your profile and forwarded to the drop shippers you are applying too. You will not have to visit each company individually and fill out hundreds of forms to setup accounts.

**Doba.ereselling.com** – Doba a trusted, proven and well established wholesale and dropship product supplier. They have currently 1,470,125 products that you can start selling immediately! The coolest part about Doba is that you don't need to have a reseller id and business licenses, they catalog all of the products. That means that you don't have to waste time signing up with 20 different drop shippers and go through all of their catalogs and apply to each company and hope to be accepted. You don't need to worry about where a product came from once you sold it, you don't have to check the stock of 20 different companies everyday to make sure they still have your products in stock.

**SaleHoo.ereselling.com** – SaleHoo is a trusted, proven and well established wholesale and dropship directory supplier. They have around 8,000 suppliers in their database that you get access too. The best part for you is that if you purchase access to this directory and you are not satisfied you can get a 100% refund so you really don't have anything to risk here.

**GovernmentAuctions.ereselling.com** - Find Government, Custom Agency, US Marshals, FBI seized property, automobiles and foreclosured houses. They have a nice searchable database for all 52 states in the United States. This is a great place to find very cheap items to resell on eBay, iOffer, Amazon, AutoTrader, etc. Massive discounts from no reserve Government Auctions - Free trial membership going on now.

## eBay Online Auction Alternatives

**eBid.ereselling.com** – eBid is a rapidly expanding new online auction marketplace that has some seriously appealing features! They have an Alexa ranking around 10k as of November, 2011 and over 4 million auctions running right now which is an insane amount. The key here is that they are spending a lot of money on advertising now and driving tons of traffic to your listings which make them a great alternative to eBay but an even better option is to use eBay with your eBid account! They have integrating features, you can import your entire eBay store to your eBid account and waaalaaaa your online! eBid lets you use their bulk upload tools so you can import your products from other marketplaces on the internet using their eBid Ninja Lister (Like Turbo Lister for eBid - sortof) and you also have the option of just importing a spreadsheet file which you can download from them for the specs required.

**uBid.ereselling.com** - uBid is an online auction marketplace, they have fabulous discounts on electronics, musical instruments and toys and games. In order to sell on their site however you need to be a serious seller with a business, it is not for your average seller listing a few products around the house. However if you can provide references and business information they are a great alternative to eBay if you have electronic products to sell.

## E-Commerce Solutions

**Bigcommerce.ereselling.com** - BigCommerce is the fastest growing ecommerce platform in the world because it provides entrepreneurs like you with an affordable, enterprise-grade ecommerce platform that's easy to manage and provides a rapid ROI!

**Vendio.ereselling.com** – Vendio is a rare breed of companies, they recently aquired one of their biggest competitors which was Andale.com and integrated the business into their own. Vendio allows eBay sellers, Amazon sellers to link all of their products together and list on both sites with marketplace integration. If you sign up with a free account you won't be able to use the eBay and Amazon features, the free version will allow you to setup a free ECommerce store with them.They recently added the ability to SELL DIRECTLY ON FACEBOOK MARKETPLACE! Which I absolutely love!

**Templates.ereselling.com** - Perfect for those who do not know how to program and create a website, no HTML knowledge really needed to use these E-Commerce templates. Design your own store with Ecommerce Templates.

## Payment Processors

**Alertpay.ereselling.com** - AlertPay is a great, trusted, and increasingly respected payment processor that had humble beginnings but is picking up. You may need an AlertPay account if you are buying wholesale world wide as they all will not accept PayPal.

**Paypal.ereselling.com** - PayPal is the obvious first choice for accepting online payments, if you don't have an account yet STOP WHAT YOUR DOING!
PayPal is owned by eBay and is accepted virtually anywhere which makes it great and popular. You can accept any type of credit card payments with ease.

**Moneybookers.ereselling.com** – Yet another up and coming payment processor, it is widely accepted internationally now and you may need it if you are buying wholesale because as previously mentioned PayPal is not always aloud.

## Hosting & Domain Names

**Hostgator.ereselling.com** – Hostgator is my absolute favorite web hosting provider, let me first say I do have a dedicated server with Godaddy as well as shared hosting plans that I have had for close to 8 years now for SEO different IP addresses. I have used HostGator side by side, usually sites that I want to build and keep I use with Hostgator because their service is absolutely phenomenal, if you call - THEY ANSWER, if you have a problem THEY FIX IT. I have never had a hosting solution that was so easy to deal with!

**Godaddy.ereselling.com** – Information about some of the cheapest hosting around, perfect for your eBay and other auction photos to include in your listings. Also offering some very cheap domain names.

## Other sites you may need.

**SquareTrade.ereselling.com** – a company that you can sign up with and put a logo on your site or listing that guarantees customer satisfaction. One of the best features of them is that you can offer your customers the ability to buy a WARRANTY! and a GUARANTEE! so they don't have to worry about damaged and defective items! They will help mediate any disputes and act as a middle man to ensure both the seller and buyer are satisfied with the transaction.

**Abebooks.ereselling.com** – If you're serious about selling books than Abebooks is the place to use, you can sell your premium top dollar books on this site better than on Amazon.

**Zazzle.ereselling.com** – It is completely free to make an account. Zazzle is definitely a leader in the game of create and print on demand products, t-shirts, mugs, art, wall accessories, electronic device accessories, cards and postage.

**Cafepress.ereselling.com** – An alternative to Zazzle

**TeraPeak.com** – The best eBay online market research tool

**Alibaba.com** – A massive directory of wholesalers world wide

www.ingramcontent.com/pod-product-compliance
Lightning Source LLC
Chambersburg PA
CBHW051448170526
45166CB00001B/155